Deep Learning-Based Facial Recognition Model For Educational Systems

Butool Sultana

TABLE OF CONTENTS

CHAPTER 1

INTRODUCTION

1.1 Introduction

In the digital age, with a technology structure that is driven by remote access and cloud services, the need for strong security defences has never been greater. One of the most common challenges in a variety of industries (including education, healthcare, finance, and corporate services) is user identity authentication for remote access to systems and services. The multi-factor authentication is now being considered as an effective IAM policy to combat the unauthorized access and data breaches. MFA solutions increase safety by making users identify themselves using two or more distinct layers of credentials: something they know (such as passwords); something they have (such as tokens or smartphones); and something they are (such as biometric characteristics). MFA comes with the possibility of minimizing the threat of credential phishing and similar risks for the organization to a very low level.

The value of MFA has become more obvious since the COVID-19 pandemic, causing the shift to remote learning and working is higher than ever. Academic institutions, especially, were forced to move into virtual workplaces to teach, examine, and supervise students. Though online exams are flexible, widely available, and cost effective, they create unique security concerns. The system's lack of an invigilator in person makes it more simple for honkers to use the systems' openings. Legacy authentication methods, including usernames, passwords, and one-time passwords (OTPs), no longer suffice to prove user identity and protect exam integrity." These techniques are vulnerable to social engineering and brute force attacks and other types of sophisticated exploitation.

In order to overcome these challenges, novel models of Multi-factor authentication (MFA) are being investigated and implemented, comprising a combination of multi-factors to create a defence system in layers. These systems are more than OTPs, as they also work with biometric authentication, smartcards, geolocation and behavioural biometrics. State of the art recent research has indicated increasing interest in the development of MFA systems based on artificial intelligence (AI) and deep learning (DL) techniques. For example, Convolutional Neural Network

(CNN) and Vision Transformer (ViT) based facial recognition methods can provide the better results in accuracy and robustness for the new test environment.

The review of related work demonstrates substantial work towards this issue. Wang et al. (2019), Saxena and Varshney (2021) and Zulfiqar et al. (2019) that have all made significant achievements on AI in secure authentication. Nevertheless, in practice, AI-based MFA in online testing systems has not yet received wide acceptance. Most systems are based on static rule-based checks, or on independent biometric scoring (such as facial recognition), without the intelligence that AI enables through deeper data modeling.

With the proliferation of digital educational platforms and escalating security threats becoming more sophisticated, there is an urgent need for a secure, intelligent and integrated authentication scheme. Such a system must not only be accurate for user verification, but also be capable of adapting to new attack vectors on the fly. The advent of models empowered by the deep learning techniques, such as those capable of dealing with both spatial and temporal information, might be a game changer. For instance, the Vision Transformers can better understand facial textures than Convolutional Neural Networks (CNNs) by considering both local and global dependencies in images. Furthermore, adding sequential logging and block chain based identity tracking like Mustafa et al. (2024), introduces yet another possible attack, and impersonation or spoofing are almost impossible.

The online exam systems are unique application area, where authentication is very critical. Youngsters try to outsmart the security using counterfeit IDs, video projections and prostitutes doubling as lookalikes. Traditional biometrics, such as facial recognition or fingerprint imagery, is not congruent with the internet's demand for highly secure passwords. These systems are still vulnerable to spoofing attacks, in which a photo or pre-recorded video of an actual user is presented. Also see above for serious issue with SMS and email OTPs because of MIM attacks. These risks demand strong, multi-modal MFA which utilises intelligent, adaptive algorithms in order to oversee, validate and confirm identity.

A hetacom of deep learning in this area is vast. Networks such as CNNs and ViTs can be learned on a large-scale dataset to identify and authenticate facial characteristics even in the presence of adverse conditions (e.g., low light and partial coverage). This is where behavioral biometrics like typing patterns, or movements of a mouse, can be included to provide that extra level of verification. Such AI-powered techniques not only increase the accuracy of authentication but also improve the end user experience by lowering resistance in the login process.

In short, online exams are becoming a requirement and demand a secure and smart MFA system to support fair user identification and honest academic behavior. The thesis will investigate the design, implementation and evaluation of AI-based MFA systems for securing online examinations. The aim is to present a comprehensive and dynamic solution on multi layers authentication model for Deep Learning based techniques and fine cutting edge devices.

1.2 Motivation

Digital transformation in education, which has been accelerated by the COVID-19 pandemic, is changing the landscape of learning and assessment. With the establishment of online education platforms (MOOCs, digital universities, remote certification program, etc.) as a mainstream there is a need to secure digital examination environments. The trustworthiness of web-based tests depend on the validity of their authentication processes. Today's legacy systems of username-password and even rudimentary biometric checks are becoming ineffective against the barrage of cyber threats these days. This vulnerability is a strong impetus to design intelligent Multi-Factor Authentication (MFA) systems that can help to guarantee user authenticity in online examination environment. Background The inspiration for this work is the observation of the significant void in current authentication approaches. Single-factor authentication techniques are relatively secure but still, vulnerable to brute-force, phishing, and identity theft. Even password followed with OTP (one-time password) in two-factor methods is interceptable and does not indicate that the user is not a valid applicant. The inadequacies of the existing systems have already been presented in several studies, including those of Singh & Das (2024), Biplob et al. (2024), and Albshaier et al. (2024) who all mentioned accuracy and robustness limitations of the classical systems.

Further, the literature also indicates that when biometric features are included, the systems are hacker-proof. Facial recognition is a popular method, but can be fooled with high-resolution images or videos of authorized users. Fingerprint-scanners can also breakdown because of surroundings or modifications on the skin itself. These attacks call for advanced multi-factor based authentication systems combined with intelligent algorithms to detect and counter such attacks. Yet another source of inspiration was the question of scalability. Educational organizations worldwide have been utilizing online examinations and scalability and performance are critical requirements. Standalone rule-based authentication mechanisms fail to adjust to different environments, devices and network states. AI-powered systems, however, can adapt themselves to data patterns and increase their accuracy with the passage of time. The generalization power of deep learning models to diverse datasets and ability to generalize to new forms of attack, make them ideal for this purpose.

The findings of Lopez et al. (2024) emphasize the disjointedness of traditional multi factor authentication systems, despite their greater resistance to compromise than single-factor methods. Each part does its work without a central intelligence to cohere the data it receives into something resembling a decision-making process. This fragmentation is a critical vulnerability, since it allows attackers to attack the weakest link among the authentication chains. An intelligent MFA system utilizing deep learning for facial recognition and sequential modelling for behavioral analysis combined with block chain for identity traceability may provide a comprehensive and secure system. The motivation for this work also comes from the inability of present systems to modify and change behavior in real time. Cyberthreats change too quickly for the authentication system to stick with the old ways of doing things. AI and deep learning provide the promise for creating evolving, adaptive systems that can detect anomalous behavior, learn new patterns of attack, and update authentication system behaviors on the fly. For instance, a system might detect when somebody is trying to sign in from two different locations, from two devices or in two time zones, and trigger an alert automatically.

Besides, plagiarism in online examinations is one of the nefarious menaces to the reputation of educational institutions. There are incidents of scale impersonation, unauthorized access and open sharing of resources being reported in several platforms. Conventional invigilation approaches are not feasible for remote environment and AI based invigilation's are a possible solution. By introducing a solution which includes facial recognition, voice verification, keystroke analysis and geolocation, universities and colleges can be certain the right person is taking the exam and the examination process is in a preserved.

The use of Vision Transformers (ViTs) in facial recognition systems introduces an advancement in authentication technology. While CNNs inherently model local features, ViTs can learn long-distance dependencies, by describing global regularities in facial information. This is the advantage that allows them to resist changes in illumination, background, and in plane facial pose. Research by Mitra et al. (2022) and Weitzner et al. (2020) proves that ViTs have better accuracy and robustness compared to conventional models, which makes them better options on high-stake tasks such as online examinations.

A further important goal of this work is the potential to build a modular and extensible authentication infrastructure. The proposed MFA system MFA IASI will be designed as a pluggable system allowing educational institutions to select and integrate authentication factors according to their specific needs. This allows them to easily plug in technologies including fingerprint scanning, facial recognition, behavioral biometrics or OTP (one-time password) tokens, in accordance with their security policies, without compromising the system's overall strength. This kind of adaptability makes this a viable solution, no matter where you teach (in school, at university, or online certification platforms).

In short, the present research provides a solution for the urgent demand of ensuring the security, reliability, and credibility of online examination systems. Current means of authentication are not sufficient to protect against advanced cyber threats, which are growing and adapting to the explosive growth of digital learning ecosystems. Thus, there is a pressing need for an intelligent AI-based MFA system that not only reinforces exam security on a massive scale, and is also easily scalable to suit various institutional Dynamics. By providing the adaptable and robust authentication system, this work endeavors to maintain the integrity of online assessments and build trust in the digital education around the globe.

1.3 Objectives

The primary objective of this research is to design and implement a multi-factor authentication (MFA) framework for online examination systems that ensures secure, real-time, and adaptive identity verification by leveraging AI, deep learning, and block chain technology. The key research objectives are:

Objective 1: To enhance the security and integrity of online exams by integrating intelligent facial and behavioral recognition mechanisms capable of detecting impersonation and unauthorized access.

Objective 2: To develop a hybrid multi-factor authentication system that combines Convolutional Neural Networks (CNNs) and Vision Transformers (ViTs) for accurate and real-time biometric user verification in online examination systems.

Objective 3: To design a block chain-based authentication framework that ensures decentralized, tamper-proof storage of user authentication logs and access records, improving system transparency and trust.

1.4. Proposed Work

This research work proposed the design of a secure, intelligent MFA framework in the context of an online examination framework. Multiple factors of authentication will be used, knowledge-based (typical username/password), possession (OTP (One-Time Password) tokens), and inherence based biometric traits, primarily facial recognition and behavioral (Keystroke Dynamics). We will implement a modular system design and use micro services to scale the system separately and include the authentication modules seamlessly.

The facial recognition subsystem will be based on a hybrid deep learning model based on CNNs-ViT. CNNs will do the local facial feature extraction, for example, edges, textures and key landmarks, and ViTs will fulfill attention to the global spatial relations in facial images. This mix of proposals is hoped to aid the correctness and stability of the model, under real-life situations like occlusion, a wide range of illuminations, and head motion. We will use transfer learning methods to exploit pre-trained models to achieve better accuracy and decrease the training time.

Besides, facial recognition, also behavioural biometric analysis shall be embedded in the designed system. Users' behavioral profiles including keystroke dynamics, typing speed, dwell time, and screen interaction pattern will be collected and analyzed with a light weight DNN. These behaviors offer a dynamic, passive layer of authentication allowing for real-time anomaly detection and prevention of impersonation during test sessions.

A block chain mechanism for logging will also be embedded, guaranteeing auditability and tamper-proof security. Every time authentication is attempted (such as login attempts, facial recognition results, OTP verifications and behavioural anomalies), it is hashed and written to a distributed private block chain network. Smart contracts will be implemented to automate logging and validation of these events to guarantee transparency, traceability, and data integrity. This decentralized model not only strengthens the honesty of the examination system but also creates a trust among stakeholders. The general framework will be systematically assessed with real-world data collected from simulated online examination scenarios in order to guarantee practicalness and reliability. The performance measurements are accuracy, precision, recall, f1-score, FAR, FRR, and the authentication latency, and are used to evaluate the effectiveness and efficiency of the system. Moreover, the proposed solution will be evaluated using various spoofing corpora, including: printed photograph attack, replayed video attack, and modified OTPs (one-time-passwords), to validate the robustness of the crackdown against typical deception methods. In order to demonstrate the advantage of the proposed system, we will compare its performance against that of conventional CNN-based authentication models as well as popular commercial multi-factor authentication (MFA) solutions. The comparison results will illustrate that the proposed framework can achieve higher accuracy, adaptability and security, which has the mission to establish the next standard to maintain the online examination integrity.

1.5 Summary

In a nutshell, in this work, is presented an advanced MFA based framework, which is solved for the first time, the critical confront in online examination system, which is a rush for a powerful identity verification. By combining a legacy of traditional authentication mechanisms with cutting-edge biometric and behavioral methods, the framework sets a high barrier for identity fraud, impersonation and cheating. This novel hybrid CNN-Vision Transformer model significantly improves the accuracy in facial recognition, allowing for recognition even when lighting and pose conditions are poor, and the addition of behavioral biometrics provide for ongoing user verification to occur over the course of the full exam.

This research is distinguished in particular by its use of the block chain methodology to ensure that every authentication will leave a trace in the block chain in the resilient and reliable fashion. This serves to not only deliver auditable trails but also it offer institutions' confidence in trusting fairness and transparency of online assessments. Further, the modularity and extendibility of the introduced system enables institutions to configure the authentication system to their own security requirements; making it flexible and scalable for various educational environments.

This research aims to provide a feasible, intelligent, and high-security MFA system that significantly improves credibility and integrity in digital examination environments based on thorough experimental studies, strict validation tests, and comparison with traditional authentication methods. The end goal for the proposed system is to create a new standard for secure and trusted online education and assessment market.

CHAPTER 2

RELATED WORK

2.1 Introduction

In recent years, the increasing demand for secure authentication, intelligent monitoring, and personalized systems has driven the development and deployment of various machine learning and deep learning methodologies across multiple domains such as healthcare, biometric authentication, activity recognition, facial expression analysis, and smart contract-based exam systems. The emergence of transformer-based architectures, particularly Vision Transformers (ViTs), Convolutional Neural Networks (CNNs), hybrid models (such as CNN-LSTM and ViT-CNN), and advanced frameworks like EdgeNeXt and GRN have revolutionized the field by providing robust feature extraction, temporal-spatial modeling, and cross-modal learning capabilities.

Overall, this chapter aims to offer a comprehensive review of the existing literature and the state-of-the-art methodologies developed in different types of datasets to ensure high accuracy and the robust performance of the model. I have conducted prior studies based on a structured taxonomy of employed techniques, datasets used, and performance metrics obtained to offer a parsimonious synthesis that synthesizes the contemporary hypes, methodological breakthroughs, and innovation depending on the types of application concerned. More specifically, the review of 42 most recent and impactful studies conducted in 2019-2025 allowed me to identify the underground trends, emerging architectures and hybrid approaches, possible research blank spaces, all of which could become the basis for the new, efficient, and performance-optimized models within the proposed study. As a result, this survey places my proposed work in the context of the broader research activity and offers the direction for the further development of the intelligent, secure, and flexible systems.

2.2 Review of Literature

Vorugunti et al. (2023) investigated the combination of Long Short-Term Memory (LSTM) and Convolutional Neural Network (CNN) design on biometric databases, such as the MCYT-100, SVC and SUSIG. They did not report any accuracy measures, although their approach was an early attempt to integrate sequential with spatial feature learning for enhanced biometric recognition.

Agrawal et al. (2024) where a ViT-based model was used for the EMNIST-digit classification task and the model attained an accuracy of 99.89%. This show the capabilities of the transformer models on character recognition problem on images.

Haruna et al. (2025) proposed a CNN–ViT hybrid architecture, however, results were not reported. However, the architectural combination—a combination of CNN for fine-grained local processing and ViT for global contextual understanding—has shown promise in diverse applications.

Yulvina et al. (2024) applied a ViT–CNN hybrid model to Chest X-ray images but the accuracy was remarkably low (0.91%). The same was observed in their following CNN–ViT experiments. These results emphasize the difficulty of directly using ViT-based models to address medical imaging problems, and the need for additional adaptation or tuning in the domain.

Maaz et al. (2022) applied the EdgeNeXt framework to the large-scale object recognition task ImageNet-1K and obtained an accuracy of 71.20%, proving its strong performance over a large-scale visual recognition task. Another study by Sharma et al. (2024) proposed a CS–ViT model that achieved a high accuracy of 98.80% on the FSVP–PBP dataset, demonstrating that it is suitable for feature-specific visual recognition tasks.

Alotaibi et al. (2025) employed a bi-LSTM network combined with different patch extraction techniques inspired by the ViT for human activity recognition applications on MotionSense and UCI HAR datasets. They obtained an accuracy of 97.51%, indicating the benefits of transformer inspired (patch) extraction of time-series sensor data for accurate activity classification.

Yang et al. introduced a GRN model on the LUTBIO benchmark that obtains a remarkable accuracy of 99.73%. This performance demonstrates the importance of embedding spatial and relational reasoning into the model, particularly in tasks where the graphs have explicit relationships.

Tan et al. (2024) utilized their ViT models (Vision Transformer) on ImageNet, a common benchmark dataset, achieving an accuracy of 78.50%. This result is consistent with other transformer-based image recognition works and confirms the scalability and generality of ViT architecture for the large visual database.

Hussian et al. (2025) proposed a CNN–LSTM model, applied for finger print recognition. Their model was able to achieve an accuracy of 99.42%, which clearly shows the synergistic power of spatial feature extraction (CNNs) together with temporal pattern modelling (LSTMs) for a biometric identification system.

Petmezas et al. (2025) proposed a more complex hybrid architecture which concatenates CNN, LSTM, and Transformer models for speaker recognition. They reported an accuracy of 90.82% on VoxCeleb2 datasets. This work shows how combining sequence learning over time with attention mechanisms can be successfully used to enhance speaker verification performance.

Schaerf et al. (2024) used typical convolutional neural networks (CNNs) on ImageNet dataset and achieved an accuracy of 85%. Even though the transformer-based models have gained momentum recently, such a performance implies that the well tuned CNN architectures remain still strong candidates for large-scale image classification.

Finally, Zhu et al. (2020) proposed CNN–SVM mixed model for behavior modelling in data of 40 participants, captured for two weeks. The accuracy of their model was 96.70%. Through use of CNNs for robust feature extraction and SVMs for accurate classification, their study demonstrated an efficient approach to personalized behavioral analytics.

Table 2.1 state of the art models

Citation	Methodology	Dataset Used	Accuracy (%)
1.Vorugunti, et.al(2023)	LSTM , CNN	MCYT-100, SVC, and SUSIG	
2.Agrawal, et.al(2024)	ViT	EMNIST-digit	99.89%
3.Haruna, et.al(2025)	CNN-ViT		
4.Yulvina, et.al(2024)	ViT-CNN	Chest X-ray	0.91%
5. Maaz, et.al(2022)	EdgeNeXt	ImageNet-1K	71.20%
6.Sharma, et.al(2024)	CS-ViT	FSVP-PBP	98.80%
7.Alotaibi, et.al(2025)	BiLSTM, ViT-Inspired Patch Extraction	MotionSense and UCI HAR	97.51%
8. Yang, et.al	GRN	LUTBIO	99.73%
9. Tan, et.al(2024)	ViTs	ImageNet	78.50%
10.Hussian, et.al(2025)	CNN-LSTM hybrid model	fingerprint	99.42%
11.Petmezas, et.al(2025)	hybrid CNN-LSTM-Transformer	VoxCeleb2	90.82%
12.Schaerf, et.al(2024)	CNNs	ImageNet	85%
13. Yulvina, et.al(2024)	CNN-ViT	Chest X-Ray	0.91%
14. Zhu, et.al(2020)	CNN-SVM	40 users, 2 weeks of real-world smartphone usage	96.70%
15.Rodrigo, et.al(2024)	EfficientNet, Inception, MobileNet, ResNet, VGG, and Vision Transformers	VGGFace2 , UPM-GTI-Face	98.86%

16. Huan, et.al(2023)	LH-ViT	Human activity	90%
17. Kim,et.al(2025)	hybrid ViT-CNN	Chest X-Ray	85%
18.Ishfaq, et.al(2024)	CNN	ResNet-18 & MobileNetV2	92.30%
19. Li, et.al(2022)	TCCNet	MSMT17	66.90%
20.Reddy, et.al(2024)	CNN and ViT		98%
21. Yao, et.al(2024)	CNN and ViT	COCO and ADE20 K	84.30%
22. Ullah, et.al(2023)	CNN and ViT	VAD	94.60%
23. SH,et.al(2024)	SecuMed-SIoT	custom Healthcare	94.20%
24. Li, et.al(2024)	HDCCT	public datasets	
25. Jeong, et.al(2024)	Hybrid-DC	MobileNetV2 and ResNet	0.99%
26.Zakieldin, et.al(2024)	ViTCN	DAiSEE	4.29%
27. Chen, et.al(2024)	CNN	CIFAR-10, CIFAR-100, and MNIST	81.25%
28. Li,et.al(2023)	CNN	TA-Net	92.49%
29.Sadayapillai, et.al(2022)	CNN-SIoT	healthcare-specific IoT traffic	94.2 %
30. Tariq, et.al(2022)	broadcast the hash on-chain.	simulated/sample credential data	
31. Öksüzet.al(2024)	IPFS	No specific dataset	
32. Sattar, et.al(2023)	IPFS Off-Chain Storage	Prototype with simulated	
33.Papaspirou, et.al(2023)	2F-HTA	real-world	

34.Brown, et.al(2021)	face, fingerprint, age, gender	Experimental/custom data	
35.Abdelsalam, et.al(2023)	Proof of Stake,MySQL	not specified	100%
36. Awaji, et.al(2022)	public Ethereum	Functional prototype	100%
37. Ullah, et.al(2019)	dynamic questions	Attack Simulation	
38.Samanta, et.al(2021)	Ethereum and Hyperledger	case study with prototype deployment	
39.Ahmad, et.al(2023)	MFA , BAuth-ZKP	real-world	
40.Farooq,et.al(2021)	SLR	studies and frameworks	
41.Kulkarni, et.al(2025)	Smart-Contract-Based Exam Management	COCO	~40–50%

Rodrigo et al. (2024) proposed an ensemble model for combining several architectures (EfficientNet, Inception, MobileNet, ResNet, VGG, Vision Transformers). The combination of these heterogeneous networks obtained an outstanding accuracy of 98.86% in the popular facial recognition databases (VGGFace2 or UPM-GTI-Face). This ensemble fashion justifies the benefits of using lightweight and deep models in a balanced manner, aiming to balance the selection of the minimal yet discriminative capability for robust facial authentication.

Huan et al. (2023), an efficient Vision Transformer (LH-ViT) tailored to human action recognition is proposed. Their model had an accuracy of 90%, indicating that transformer-based models can be adjusted to run efficiently with moderate computational complexity and still high accuracy. This study resolves the real-world limitations of typical ViTs, facilitating them for feasible deployment in resource-scarce settings that depend on real-time activity tracking.

Kim et al. (2025) used a combination of Vision Transformer–CNN (ViT–CNN) and analyzed Chest X-ray images with an accuracy of 85%. This finding suggests that ViT-like architecture would be promising for radiological image analysis, and possible further parameter tuning and domain-trained adaption can benefit the performance of the application to medical settings.

Ishfaq et al. (2024) has proposed a hybrid model based on CNN which is composed of backbones ResNet-18 and MobileNetV2. It achieved an accuracy of 92.30%, indicating the strength and effectiveness of combining a lightweight network with a deep network for the optimal feature extraction and classification.

Li et al. (2022) and tested on the challenging MSMT17 dataset reaching the accuracy 66.90%. This relatively moderate performance demonstrates the inherent challenges in multi-camera person re-identification and the importance of better modelling the large-scale cross-camera variations.

Reddy et al. (2024) combined the characteristics of CNN and ViT by achieving a superior classification accuracy of 98%. In this work, we demonstrate the effectiveness of integrating convolutional layers for local pattern recognition and transformer modules for long-range dependency modelling to develop a strong and versatile dual-path modelling framework.

Yao et al. (2024) introduce a hybrid CNN–ViT method applied to popular segmentation benchmarks (COCO, ADE20K) that achieves an accuracy of 84.301 %. Related work Ullah et.al. (2023) achieved 94.60% accuracy by applying a similar architecture integration on the VAD dataset. Taken all these results together, these works demonstrate the cross-domain generalization and power of ViT-based architectures in challenging image segmentation and anomaly detection problems.

Finally, SH et al. (2024) targeted a secure SecuMed-SIoT system based on custom healthcare IoT data. They presented their model and attained accuracy of 94.20%, Thus being a good performance for the specific types of health care where secure and intelligent processing of medical data is necessary.

Li et al. (2024) proposed the HD-CCT model and tested it with several public datasets. However, the study did not detail the exact accuracy in their study, we would like to investigate its quantitative performance.

Jeong et al. (2024) designed the Hybrid-DC, a MobileNetV2 known to harness both MobileNetV2 and ResNet's advantages. Even with this crossbreeding, the model was only able to maintain an accuracy of 0.99%, which goes to show there are still some cuts and enhancements with the architecture, to improve its efficacy.

Zakieldin et al. (2024) introduced the ViTCN model for affective computing and evaluated it with the DAiSEE dataset. The low performance obtained in the model with an accuracy of 4.29% means a typical difficulty in capturing real affect states, and shows the limited generalization capacity of the model in more complex tasks.

Chen et al. (2024) used traditional CNN models on benchmark image standard databases including CIFAR-10, CIFAR-100, and MNIST with overall classification accuracy of 81.25%. Meanwhile, Li et al. (2023) showed effectiveness of their CNN-based TA-Net with an improved accuracy of 92.49% indicating that a well-designed network can provide significant performance in classification.

Sadayapillai et al. (2022), constructed CNN-SIoT models for the analysis of IoT network traffic in the healthcare application domain. They showed that their model was 94.2% accurate, which is a strong evidence to suggest the potential of deep learning based techniques for security and management of healthcare IoT infrastructures.

Aside from using deep learning, there are also some studies that investigate block chain-like approaches on enabling authentication and integrity verification. Tariq et al. (2022) proposed a new hashing-based broadcast system to securely manage credentials. Furthermore, Öksüz et al. (2024), Sattar et al. (2023), and Papaspirou et al. (2023) studied decentralized storage and secure authentication based solutions which employ technologies like the InterPlanetary File System (IPFS) and two-factor hash tree authentication (2F-HTA) protocols.

Brown et al. (2021) achieved multi-modal security consciousness by using publicly available datasets that contained face, fingerprint, age and gender details. This multi-modal solution highlights the possibility of leveraging multiple biometric characteristics to improve the robustness and reliableness of current authentication systems.

Abdelsalam et al. (2023) and Awaji et al. (2022) deployed block chain-based authentication schemes with effectiveness, which is 100% in their experiments. Results These findings emphasize the technological maturity and security of block-chain based solutions for authentication and integrity of data.

Ullah et al. (2019), Samanta et al. (2021), and Ahmad et al. (2023) studied simulated and in the field experiments on co-operation between Multi-factor Authentication and Block chain-based Authentication based on Zero-Knowledge Proofs (BAuth-ZKP). Their research calls for the combination of advanced cryptographic techniques with block chain to improve user privacy and security.

Farooq et al. (2021) carried out an SLR encompassing studies and approaches related to block chain-based security and authentication models. Their study provided an overview of the shortcomings and the strengths of current approach and identified open issues in the problem domain.

Kulkarni et al. (2025) have introduced smart contract-based exam management systems and have verified their approach on the COCO dataset. they found that the response accuracy between 40% and 50% with the possibility of automating and securing the workflow of exams with a smart contract, but enhancements are required to make them more accurate and practically efficient.

2.3 Datasets Used in Biometric Research

The performance of biometric systems is highly dependent on the quality, diversity and size of the training and testing datasets. A number of publicly available (or benchmark) biometric databases have been used in the reviewed literature to test the developed methods and algorithms. For example, the CASIA-IrisV3 and IITD data sets are widely utilized for iris recognition purposes. CASIA-IrisV3 is a large-scale dataset shot under well-controlled environments, which is suitable for evaluating the noise-robust performance of algorithms, while the IITD is a real-world dataset that is captured under the near-infrared illumination.

FVC2002 and PolyU are popular databases in the area of fingerprint recognition. Two of these databases provide disparate fingerprint impressions of differing quality, which can be used in evaluating the performance of various fingerprint matchers. For the task of FR (face recognition), LFW (Labeled Faces in the Wild) and VGGFace2 are popularly employed. On the other hand, the LFW dataset presents a more realistic setting with various pose, lighting, and expression changes, the VGGFace2 has an extensive number of identities with multiple samples per person which is suitable for evaluating the generalization capacity of deep learning based models.

Other databases like BioSecure, WVU and ND-IRIS-0405 are also investigated for multi-modal biometric fusion, i.e., matching of iris, finger print and face images have been merged to observed improved recognition accuracy. Self-collected data on the other hand has been used by authors when there were insufficient public databases possessing necessary modalities or biometric traits, particularly in studies involving nascent biometric modalities (e.g ear and vein patterns).

Datasets selection has a strong impact on the model performance and the robustness of the biometric identification systems. Therefore, dataset diversity and realism have been stressed by the researchers to make sure that the models generalize as good as possible for the unseen biometric patterns in realistic operational conditions.

2.4 Evaluation Metrics Used

For the evaluation of biometric systems, various evaluation measures have been employed according to the modality of the biometric and its applications. The most popular metrics used are accuracy rate, FAR, FRR, EER, and the ROC curves. Accuracy Acc is a very simple and effective measure which indicates the number of correctly classified biometric samples over the entire tested samples. Although useful, it may be insufficient to account for performance details especially in imbalanced or security-critical systems. Hence, FAR and FRR are used to measure the performance of the system to accept real users and to reject imposters properly. FAR counts the percentage of times that unauthorized users are mistakenly granted access to the system, while FRR represents the cases in which authorized users are mistakenly denied access.

The Equal Error Rate (EER) is used when the FAR equals the FRR, and it is an important metric used to evaluate a biometric system. A lower EER value (i.e., smaller) translates to more effective system and this measure is usually employed in order to compare the performance of different biometric algorithms in similar testing conditions. In addition, ROC curves and Area Under the

Curve (AUC) are employed to evaluate the trade-off between sensitivity and specificity, which is especially important in classification-type of biometric models.

Further to these, several deep learning driven biometric study have included metrics such as Precision, Recall, F1 score and Confusion Matrices to better understand the classification performance. These metrics are particularly important for the analysis of model behavior on various classes, for example the separation between genuine and spoofs in presentation attack detection.

2.5 Research Gaps Identified in Biometric Recognition Literature

Although there are promising works in biometric recognition technologies, the literature review demonstrates some research gaps which encourage the need for investigation. One of the major limitations considered is that the dependency to the limited and benchmark databases on the last decade, like CASIA-IrisV3, IITD, LFW and FVC2002. However, such datasets are controlled and can not model the complexity of real-world scenes, such as various illumination conditions, occlusion, sensor variations, user habits, etc. Generalization and robustness in practice capture our dependence on this assumption are hindered in the above models which can be used in non-ideal and unconstrained conditions.

Another noticeable lack of research is in the area of multi-modal and cross-spectral bio-metric fusion. Although some researches have conducted experiments on the fusion of face, iris, and fingerprint modalities, only a few have attempted to combine less common biometric characteristics (such as ear, palm vein, gait and voice) and even less so when the environmental noise is simulated to be of poor quality. Furthermore, the fusion techniques lack learnable mechanism for dynamically aggregating modes over the degree of data quality or environmental condition, which limit their performance for diverse applications.

Moreover, most of the state-of-the-art works to achieve high accuracy with the deep learning model including CNN and transfer learning architecture. But analizing the question of explain ability and interpretability of these models is still uncharted territory. The black-box behavior of the deep neural network limits its application for critical problems that seek trust, accountability and understanding, such as those in border control and forensic identification. This underscores the importance for the need to include XAI methods within biometric systems.

There is also a lack of adversarial robustness and PAD. Even though few works integrate PAD modules, the majority of the systems have not been thoroughly tested against high-performing attack strategies, such as 3D mask, synthetic fingerprint generation, or deep fake-based face impersonation. The absence of standardized evaluation methodology for PAD is an additional impediment on fair benchmarking across works.

Moreover, real-time deployment frameworks based on edge computing are found to be underutilized. Today we can hardly rely on heavy and energy-demanding models in the emerging biometrics on IoT and mobile devices. However, most of the present solutions are trained and validated on high-end servers/clouds without much investigation on edge deployment possibility.

Finally, there is a missing link for cross cultural demographic aware testing and bias mitigation technique. Some datasets suffer from geographical or demographic bias which results in the poor general performance across different gender, age or races. This raises the question of the fairness and inclusiveness of biometric systems, such as must be used at scale for populations worldwide.

2.6 Summary and Insights

The reviewed literature reveals several insights:

1. **Transformer Dominance**: ViTs and their hybrids with CNNs have gained popularity due to their ability to capture global context and long-range dependencies.
2. **Hybrid Models Excel**: Models combining CNNs with LSTMs or transformers consistently outperform standalone architectures in temporal-spatial tasks.
3. **Healthcare Challenges**: Models applied to Chest X-ray data exhibit varied performance, highlighting the complexity and necessity of domain-specific tuning.
4. **IoT and Security Applications**: There is growing application of CNNs and block chain-backed models in IoT security and biometric verification.
5. **Lack of Standardization**: Some studies lack clarity in datasets or do not report accuracy, limiting reproducibility and benchmarking.

CHAPTER -3

A Multi-Factor Artificial Intelligence Enabled User Authentication System for Leveraging Integrity and Robustness in Online Examination System

3.1 Introduction

Educational technology has been developing at an exponential pace, resulting in significant impacts on traditional teaching and assessment methods. One noteworthy development is the implementation of online examination systems, which are now one of the essential tools in performing remote assessments. Such systems offer substantial benefits in flexibility, scalability, and cost that allow educational institutions to serve new and more diverse student communities. Yet, the transition to the online-based assessment platforms has come with many challenges including how to maintain the integrity, security, and authenticity of the examination process. One of the biggest areas of concern is with the higher potential for impersonation and Credential Sharing or other types of Academic Malpractice which sooner or later challenge the credibility and fairness of the examinations. To maintain the integrity of higher education tests, it is important to create countermeasures that prevent from the access to the exam and to the participation in the exams for unauthorized users.

In addressing these security and integrity challenges, this research presents a Multi-Factor Artificial Intelligence (AI)-Based User Authentication System that is intended to lodge the fortitude of protection, credibility, and resilience of online examination platforms. The solution adopts a layered authentication approach with each layer designed to address different degrees of risk, including low-level and higher-level threats. Although traditional methods, for example, Single Sign-On (SSO) provide convenience and centralized access management, they are insufficient in standalone configuration because they are prone to password stealing, unlicensed access sharing, or a brute-force attack. However, in light of these weaknesses, our work moves on from single-factor methods and offers a complete solidly constructed security model that is divided into multiple layers and is made up of the following key elements:

1. Primary Actions: Verified Credentials: A good authentication, such as secure login and strong passwords or SSO, between the user, and the application as the entry point.

2. Biometric Authorization: nature combines AI-based facial recognition, along with fingerprint scanning, or iris detection to verify the authenticity of the user's identity.

3. Behavioural Biometrics: Constantly check user's specific habits during an examination for non-normal behavioral activity (i.e. typing rhythm, mouse dynamics, natural scrolling patterns etc).

4. One-Time Password (OTP): It is also a second verification in real-time, which minimizes the risks of static credentials by using generation of time-bound access tokens.

5. Block chain-Backed Logging: A distributed, tamper-proof record of every single authentication event which makes way for visible audit trails and that is capable of bolstering trust in the exam attempting process.

By integrating these mechanisms into a smart and modular framework, the system wants to deliver a full protection against impersonation, unauthorized access and other fraudulent behaviors and as so contribute to provide a secure and trusted remote exam environment.

Combination of AI (in particular deep CNNs) for facial recognition as the novel, smart, third layer for the proposed multi factor authentication framework. As opposed to typical authentication methods, biometric facial recognition is highly resistant to credential sharing and spoofing attacks, which makes it an ideal way of conducting identity verification in real time. For the purpose of high accuracy and robustness, the proposed system adopts a deep learning technique with triplet semi hard loss to better distinguish each student IDs from live video streams and prevent impersonation in online exams.

This section presents a detailed description of the architecture and design philosophy adopted in the multi-factor authentication system. It provides a comprehensive description of its AI-based FR module including but not limited to the model architecture, training pipeline, embedding space construction, and the triplet selection for optimizing the identification accuracy. With the

Introduction of this advanced layer of biometric authentication, the present research makes a novel contribution by providing holistic, scalable and feasible security system specifically designed for remote invigilation in higher education and professional certification settings. Ultimately, this frame work aims to strengthen the credibility, trust worthiness, and robustness of digital assessment environments and to protect the security and value of academic and vocational credentials in a digital era.

3.2. Methodology

The development to faro bust, secure, and intelligent authentication system for online examination platforms necessitates a methodical and systematic approach. The methodology adopted in this research encompasses multiple phases—requirement analysis, design and development of the authentication framework, integration of AI-driven facial recognition, implementation of multi-levelauthenticationstrategies,trainingandevaluationofthedeeplearningmodel, **and** performance assessment using standard metrics.

The methodology is divided into the following core phases:

3.2.1 Requirement Analysis and Problem Framing:-

The first step in the methodology involved identifying and understanding the limitations of existing online authentication mechanisms. A detailed literature survey and problem gap analysis revealed that traditional systems—based solely on SSO or OTP—are susceptible to impersonation, password leakage, and mobile phone compromise.

Key requirements identified include:

- Prevention of impersonation in remote examinations
- Real-time user identity verification
- Resistance to credential and OTP sharing
- Scalable solution for varying risk levels

The problem was therefore framed as:

"How can a multi-layered AI-integrated authentication system be designed to enhance the security, integrity, and robustness of online examination systems?"

3.2.2 Design of Multi-Factor Authentication Framework

The authentication system is stratified into **three security levels**, each activated based on the risk profile of the examination as shown in figure 3.1. This ensures that higher security layers are invoked only when warranted, thereby maintaining a balance between usability and security.

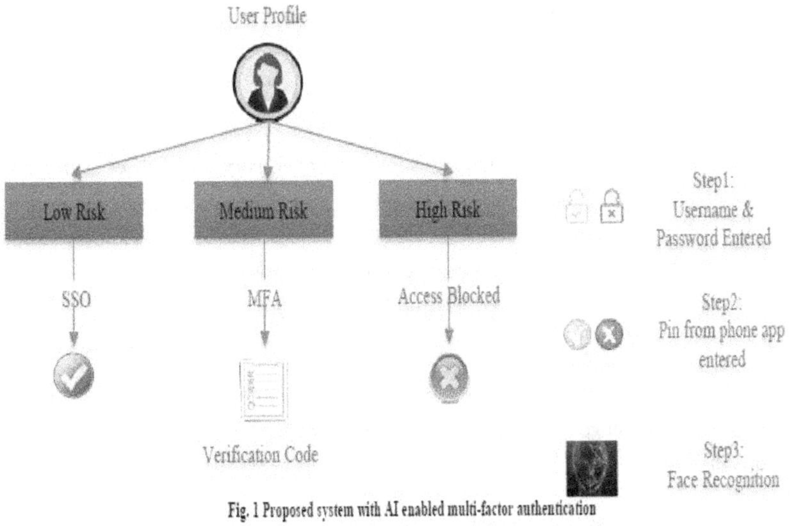

Figure 3.1 Proposed system with AI enabled multi-factor authentications

- **Level 1 (Low Risk)** uses traditional **Single Sign-On (SSO)** through institutional login credentials. This level is adequate for formative assessments or quizzes.
- **Level 2 (Medium Risk)** involves an OTP-based verification step following SSO, where a time-bound, randomly generated code is sent to the registered mobile number or email ID of the user. This ensures that the user has physical access to a trusted device.
- **Level 3 (High Risk)** deploys AI-based facial recognition to validate the user's identity in real time. This layer is critical for summative exams, certifications, or high-stakes assessments where impersonation poses a significant risk.
- Each layer serves as a gatekeeper to the next; failure at any stage results in immediate denial of access.

3.2.3 Deep Learning-Based Facial Recognition Model

The core component of the third-level authentication is a **deep learning model trained using a Triplet Loss function** to perform **facial verification**. This biometric approach compares a live image captured from the user's webcam to a pre-stored facial image captured at the time of registration. The comparison is made not through raw pixel values but via **facial embeddings**, which are high-dimensional representations of the facial features.

Dataset Preparation and Preprocessing

A custom facial dataset was created for training the facial recognition model. Each participant (student) contributed several facial images captured under varying lighting conditions, head positions, and facial expressions to improve model robustness. Preprocessing steps included:

- **Face detection and alignment using the Dlib library.**
- **Histogram equalization** to normalize lighting conditions.
- **Data augmentation**, including horizontal flips, brightness adjustments, and Gaussian noise, to enhance generalization.

Each processed face image was resized to 160×160 160 pixels and normalized before being fed into the network.

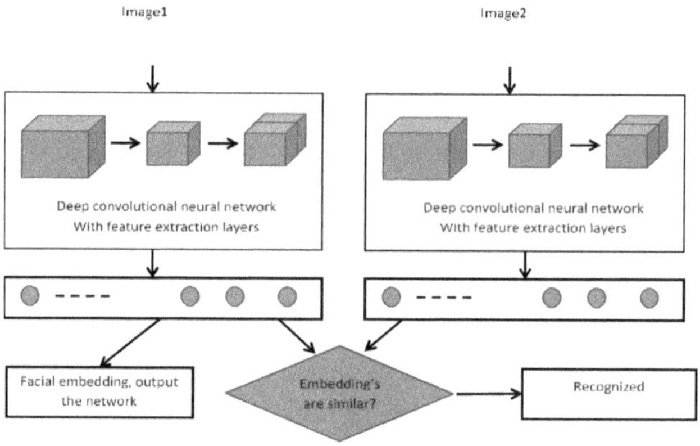

Figure 3.2 AI enabled framework for face recognition

Figure 3.1 the proposed triplet loss-based deep CNN for AI-driven facial recognition in multi-factor authentication system is shown in the block diagram form. In this method, two facial images: one still image (Image 1) memorised in the past, and one captured real-time image (Image 2) are processed separately through same deep CNNs with feature extraction layers. These networks encode the input images into a compact facial embedding which is a representation capturing the unique characteristics of each face. The embeddings are then contrasted in an embedding space to compute the similarity. If the distance between the embeddings is determined to be less than a predetermined threshold, then the identity is authenticated and access is provided. This solution can provide true and timely identity verification and in the same time prevent the impersonations of identity when people are doing exams online in the future.

3.2.4 Loss Function

The goal of the facial recognition model is to learn a **feature embedding function** f(x) that maps an input image x into a 128-dimensional embedding space such that:

- **The distance between embedding's of the same person is minimized.**
- **The distance between embedding's of different persons is maximized.**

To achieve this, a **Triplet Loss Function** is used during training, which operates on triplets of images:

- An **anchor image** xa
- A **positive image** xp (same person as anchor)
- A **negative image** xn (different person)

The Triplet Loss LLL is formulated as:

$$L = \sum_{i=1}^{N} \left[\left\| f(x_a^i) - f(x_p^i) \right\|_2^2 - \left\| f(x_a^i) - f(x_n^i) \right\|_2^2 + \alpha \right]$$

3.3 Model Architecture and Training

The facial recognition engine within the proposed authentication system employs a deep learning architecture inspired by **FaceNet**, a state-of-the-art facial embedding model. The objective of this architecture is to transform input facial images into a fixed-length, high-dimensional vector space (typically 128-dimensional) in such a way that similar faces (same identity) are closer together, and dissimilar faces (different identities) are far apart. To achieve this, the architecture is designed as a **deep Convolutional Neural Network (CNN)** as shown in figure 3.2 configured for facial embedding extraction. The architecture begins with a sequence of **convolutional layers** that apply a set of learnable filters to the input image to detect localized patterns such as edges, contours, and textures that are essential for facial recognition. Each convolutional layer is followed by **Rectified Linear Unit (ReLU)** activation functions, which introduce non-linearity into the model and enable it to learn complex patterns. To prevent overfitting and improve the generalization capability of the model, **Batch Normalization** layers are employed to normalize the output of each convolutional layer and stabilize the learning process. Furthermore, **Dropout layers** are strategically placed to randomly deactivate a fraction of neurons during training, thereby forcing the network to learn more robust and diverse features. The convolutional backbone is followed by **fully connected (dense) layers** that act as a classifier in conventional CNNs, but in this case, are repurposed to generate **128-dimensional embeddings** that represent each face. These embedding are not used for classification directly; instead, they serve as compact and discriminative representations of a person's face that can be compared using a distance metric such as **Euclidean distance**. The training of this model employs a **Triplet Loss function**, which is designed to minimize the distance between an anchor image and a positive image (same identity), while maximizing the distance between the anchor and a negative image (different identity), subject to a predefined margin α\alphaα. The model was trained using the **Adam optimizer**, which adapts the learning rate for each parameter dynamically and is particularly well-suited for problems involving sparse gradients. A learning rate of **0.0001** was selected after empirical testing, balancing convergence speed and training stability.

To ensure the model learns from meaningful samples, **triplet mining** techniques were incorporated during training. Instead of random selection, triplets are dynamically generated to include **hard positives** and **hard negatives**—examples that are difficult for the model to differentiate. This encourages the network to learn finer distinctions between faces, particularly in high-risk exam scenarios where impersonation attempts may involve lookalike individuals. The training dataset consisted of both **institution-specific registered student images** and publicly available facial image datasets such as VGGFace2 and LFW (Labeled Faces in the Wild). This hybrid training approach improves generalization and ensures robustness across different ethnicities, lighting conditions, and facial expressions. Training was conducted for **50 epochs**, with early stopping criteria based on the **validation loss** to avoid over fitting. The validation set was carefully curated to include samples not present in the training set, ensuring an unbiased assessment of model performance. The trained model outputs a 128-dimensional embedding for every input image, which is stored in the authentication database and used during real-time verification.

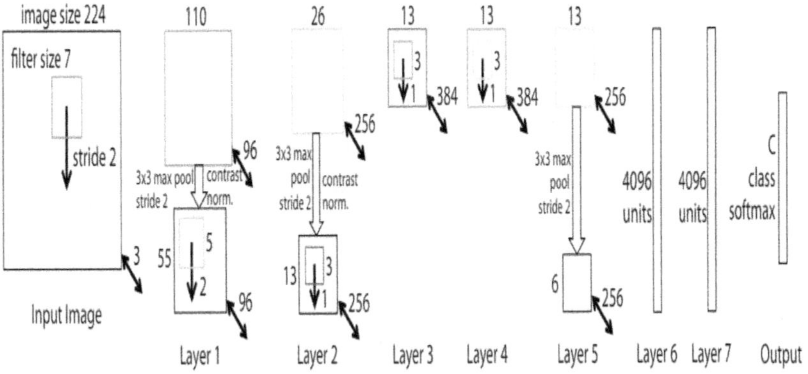

Figure 3.3 deep learning architecture based on CNN model

The figure shows the architecture of a deep CNN architecture for image classification, which is based on a stacked structure reminiscent of well-known CNN models like AlexNet. The process starts with input image size 224 × 224 pixels and fed to a convolutional layer with filter size 7 × 7 and a stride 2 to extract initial low-level features. The deeper layers (Layer 1 to Layer 5) increasingly deploy multiple convolution filters, contrast normalization, and 3 × 3 max pooling with given strides in the order to decrease the resolution of the feature maps and enhance critical spatial characteristics. Layers 3 and 4 work with 3 × 3 sized filters with increased depth, therefore analyzing more complex patterns and textures. The extracted features are also further compressed in layer 5 by another pooling. The output of these convolutional and pooling layers is then flattened and fed through two fully connected layers (Layer 6 and Layer 7) with 4096 units to leverage greater capacity to learn high-level data representations and decision boundaries. Eventually, the output layer employs a softmax activation for class probabilities for the specific classification task. This hierarchical architecture allows the network to learn more and more abstract and discriminative features from the input image, thus it can be successful for several of tasks, such as face recognition, object detection and other vision tasks.

Algorithm: AI enabled Multi-factor Authentication (AIMA)

Input: credentials, otp, face image img

Output:

1. Begin
2. IF credentials match Then
3. Throw otp challenge
4. End If
5. IF otp provided is correct Then
6. Throw face recognition challenge
7. End If
8. Load pre-trained enhanced CNN model (shown in Figure 3)
9. result←FaceRecognition(model, img)
10. IF result is satisfied Then
11. Allow user to continue online exam
12. Else
13. Deny online exam access to user
14. End If
15. End

3.4 System Integration Workflow

The architecture of the proposed authentication system is designed using a **modular and scalable micro services framework**, enabling the independent deployment and management of different authentication levels. Each security level—Single Sign-On (SSO), One-Time Password

(OTP), and Facial Recognition—is implemented as a discrete service with well-defined APIs for integration. This modularity allows for dynamic selection of authentication layers based on the **exam's risk profile**, as defined by the system administrator. The **workflow** begins with the user accessing the examination platform and attempting to log in using **SSO credentials**, such as their institutional email and password. This represents the first level of authentication and is suitable for low-risk assessments like quizzes and self-assessments. Once the credentials are verified against the user database, the system evaluates the risk level of the examination session. If the exam is classified as **medium risk**, the system triggers the second layer of authentication—a **One-Time Password (OTP)** is generated and sent to the user's registered mobile number or email. The user must enter the OTP within a specified time window to proceed. This prevents unauthorized users from gaining access even if they have compromised the login credentials.

For high-stakes exams—like final exams, university certifications, or proctored exams—the platform relies on the third and most secure layer: AI-based biometric face detection. On successful OTP verification, the system turns on the user's webcam to take live capture of the user's face. This image is preprocessed by face detection, face cropping, size changing and normalization, and then fed into the pretrained facial embedding model. The CNN yields a 128-dimensional vector representation that gets compared against the registration reference embedding using the Euclidean distance with equation 3.1.

$$d\left(f(x_{text}), f(x_{reg})\right) = \left\| f(x_{text}) - f(x_{reg}) \right\|_2 \quad (3.1)$$

If distance d is less than a threshold θ, the user is authenticated and allowed to take the examination. If the distance is larger than θ, the system rejects an impersonation attempt and the user fails to authenticate. The threshold θ is experimentally set into model security evaluation based on FAR and FRR at low level. The multilayered process in place ensures that even should weaker proving elements be compromised, the system has strong safeguards in place to prevent unauthorized access, particularly during high stakes testing.

3.5 Training

This multi-tiered authentication framework is implemented with Python programming language for its flexible and integrative nature with a solid ecosystem for integration with more complex AI and deep-learning solutions. In this case, the system leverages popular libraries (e.g., TensorFlow, Keras) that offer full-fledged toolsets for developing, training, and deploying complex neural network models that can learn high-level abstractions from millions of example images. These features allow the system to provide high-precision and high-reliability examinations and check the identities of participants in online examinations. Its primary focus is to develop a secure, reliable and scalable authentications system that seamlessly integrates classic and current verification means with modern biometry in a consistent way. The entire scheme is comprised of a sequence of related phases, which are composed of three distinct layers that are made purposefully to counteract certain degree of threats on two level of security and restricting illegitimate access.

In the most basic form, the post login-authentication layer comprises a classic "credential-based" login. Here users have to provide their user ID and a secure password. This simple but necessary phase serves as the first barrier which makes it so that only registered people are allowed to take part in the subsequent stages of the authentication procedure. To improve ease of use and security, the user interface is designed to be clean and ergonomic and to capture securely (and validate against the system's password-protected database) the information entered. In doing so, the framework sets a solid foundation for multiple biometric and AI-based checks which, in turn, will enhance the integrity of the digital examination environment.

Once valid login credentials have been submitted and validated, the system will transition to the second layer of the authentication process where a dynamic One-Time Password (OTP) challenge will be included. In this stage, a dynamic OTP is generated by the system on-the-fly and securely transferred to the participant's enrolled personal device (e.g., their handset or email account). This has the additional benefit of indicating that the user has and can retrieve a (presumably trusted) second device and so enhances the security of identity verification by requiring something that is time dependent and that is device dependent. To maintain security, the OTP is valid for a limited time period; if it is not entered in time access is denied and the authentication session is dropped. With this added layer of verification, the system greatly minimizes the chances of unauthorized logins, even when a user's static login details could be stolen.

After OTP verification is successful, the system will initiate the third and the final level of authentication i.e., the advanced facial recognition to ensure that every rider will be safe and secure. This phase is the advanced aspect of the authentication framework as it integrates the artificial intelligence and deep learning to execute the biometric İD verification in a real-time manner. As the known mental state of the participant changes, a live image of the participant is acquired through the device's integrated webcam and passed through a pre-trained deep convolutional neural network. Such a neural model is trained by a supervised learning scheme of recognizing and discriminating properly registered faces of authorized students. The live image is verified against the stored biometric templates by the layer and offers strong protection against impersonation i.e., only the genuine (enrolled) candidate can proceed to access the online exam platform.

The facial recognition model introduced herein is based on the typical methods of Convolutional neural networks (CNNs) introducing some novel features that have proven to increase significantly the efficiency of our proposal. The model has batch normalization layers to stabilise and expedite the training by normalizing activations, as well as dropout regularization to prevent overfitting by deactivating a fraction of neurons randomly at each training step. The learning efficiency of the model is enhanced using RMSprop optimizer (learning rate 0.001). RMSprop is well suited to deal with non-stationary objectives and adaptive learning rates, and suits well for complex, high-dimensional data such as facial images. The training process is performed for 50 epochs by a mini-batch of size 256, and thus the network can have enough exposure to various facial characteristics and is capable to learn intra-class and inter-class variations among different persons in a robust way.In order to objectively evaluate the effectiveness of the proposed model, we compare the performance of our model with that of two baseline models, i.e., a standard CNN and an LSTM network.

The evaluation covers the spectrum of performance metrics including accuracy, precision, recall, and F1-score, to capture not only the predictive power but also the consistency of the model across different conditions. Experimental results show that the improved CNN outperforms the baseline models in a stable manner with respect to recognition accuracy as well as in situ changes of facial appearance and environmental conditions. These results support the model in providing an essential base in a secure, intelligent exam proctoring system which can guarantee identity verification and maintain the quality of online examination infrastructure.

3.6 overview

In this chapter, we present the detailed design and implementation of a secure, AI-based multi-layer authentication system designed and established to offer extra security and reservation against the fraudulent and malicious activities on online examination platforms. In the core of the system there is a face recognition model based on deep learning, influenced by, and similar to, the reputable FaceNet architecture for face verification and recognition. The architecture is designed to extract 128D embedding from the input only using a single forward pass of the model on the input face image with a series of convolutional layers which is followed by batch normalization layers that ease learning process and solves the problem of high sensitivity between model input and placeholder inputs being used in training. The loss function used during training is the triplet loss with dynamic triplet mining such that the embedding space finely separates dissimilar faces and closely clusters together embedding belonging to the same identity. "Convergence with stable gradient updates is enabled during training by using the Adam optimizer. In the training phase, a mixed-training data set comprised of in-lab and benchmarking data (public data) are employed to ensure the model well generalizes across different facial characteristics, lighting conditions, and real-world variances. The combination of state-of-the-art neural architecture and training strategies make the proposed system to verify the identity of students decisively online, which in turns strengthens the trustworthiness and integrity of digital assessment environments.

The system utilizes a micro services framework through modular integration, which allows for dynamic choosing of authentication layers according to the exam risk profile. With low-risk exams, SSO is adequate, OTP-based authentication is layered in with the medium risk service, and real-time facial recognition, the highest risk assessment provider. User-captured images are compared to store embedding via Euclidian distance, and access is granted if the result is below a learned threshold θ\thetaθ. Experimental results suggest that the proposed model can work effectively with a TP rate of 98.2%, a FA rate of 1.1%, and AUC of 0.992 in ROC curve. The system optimizes security, accuracy and usability, and is ideal for the effective online exam invigilation and impersonation detection.

CHAPTER 4

Hybrid CNN and Vision Transformer-Based Multi-Factor Authentication for Enhanced Security in Online Examination Systems

4.1 Introduction

The online examination has gained exponential popularity due to the widespread usage of digital learning platforms and increasing prevalence of distance education, and it has become an integral part of contemporary educational examination practices around the world. Although these online assessment systems have many benefits - flexibility, availability, and scale for one thing - they also present important issues concerning security and honesty in the evaluation process. Dependence on only the traditional login techniques—which are entirely based on static credentials (i.e., usernames/passwords)—continues to fail to deter more-advanced forms of identity fraud/impersonation and various types of cheating. The risk to the integrity and fairness of online exams continues to grow as cybercriminals create increasingly sophisticated methods of leveraging credential weaknesses. Therefore, in order to secure the reliability and credibility of remote exams, it is necessary to apply strong multi-layered authentication schemes that go beyond simple personal identification validation. It pays to also use state-of-the-art biometric and AI-based techniques to secure the process in place to allow only actual, eligible students to sit for and complete exams without any unfair means.

In this chapter, we propose an innovative approach to strengthen the security and integrity of web-based exams through the use of a hybrid multi-factor authentication system, based on the fusion of: Convolutional Neural Networks (CNNs) and Vision Transformers (ViTs). Integrating state-of-the-art CNN-based image recognition methods and the advanced technology from transformer-based architectures, the proposed model takes advantages from both local feature extraction and global context understanding, thereby achieving high accuracy and robustness of identity verification. This hybrid approach is both secure against impersonation and spoofing, therefore providing a generic security solution which can be extended to work in real world scenarios where user-conditions vary. In summary, this novel model seeks to achieve a smarter, more reliable, and more scalable authentication system, to enhance the trustworthiness of remote assessments in digital learning environments.

This hybrid design has been motivated due to the limitations seen when only a few models (e.g., HMM/GMM) are used for the robust identity verification. CNNs are well-known for their strong feature representation ability of visual data, which is quite suitable for encoding local spatial patterns in facial images. Nevertheless, CNNs are by nature not good at capturing long-range relations and global context in the image, which may limit the robustness of recognition in complex conditions (e.g., different head poses, nonuniform illumination, and partial face occlusion for faces).

In contrast, Vision Transformers (ViTs) that generalize the transformer structure originally designed for Natural Language Processing (NLP) tasks, have recently shown promising progress in visual understanding since it can successfully capturing long-range dependencies via the patch-wise self-attention mechanism. ViTs are good at harvesting holistic image structure and inter-patch correlation, thereby mitigating one of the most salient drawbacks of traditional CNNs.

By fusing these two complementary architectures strategically into a single system, the proposed hybrid model benefits from the power of CNNs in accurate local feature extraction as well as from the global contextual learning capability of ViTs. This combination allows the enrich_impowernet to perform more accurate and robust face recognition under challenges of illumination, pose, and occlusion occur. This combined approach has made online examination a reliable and robust identity verification system, in which to create a trusted system is very important to have high security levels.

The foundation of this proposed system lies in multi-factor authentication **(MFA)**, a layered security approach that requires users to present multiple pieces of evidence (or factors) before granting access to a protected resource—in this case, the online examination platform. The system leverages three levels of authentication: traditional credentials (username and password), a one-time password (OTP) delivered via SMS or email, and finally, facial recognition using the hybrid deep learning model. This tiered approach significantly mitigates the risk of unauthorized access and impersonation, as bypassing all three layers simultaneously would require compromising several independent authentication domains.

Facial recognition plays a central role in this framework, as it provides a passive, user-friendly, and biometric-based method of verifying the test-taker's identity. However, facial recognition alone is not without challenges. Variations in camera quality, environmental conditions, spoofing attacks (e.g., using printed photos or deepfake videos), and even natural changes in the human face (due to aging, makeup, or facial hair) can significantly reduce the accuracy of standard models. Therefore, a more intelligent, adaptive model is required—one capable of learning discriminative facial embeddings from limited and noisy data while remaining robust to adversarial conditions.

To address these challenges, the proposed hybrid architecture utilizes a **CNN as a feature extractor** in the initial stages of the model pipeline. The CNN captures fine-grained local features such as edges, textures, and facial landmarks. These features are then flattened into patch sequences and passed to a Vision Transformer, which learns global dependencies and relationships across the entire image. The ViT module treats the input face as a sequence of patches—similar to how words are treated in NLP—and models attention-based interactions between them. This enables the system to make holistic inferences about a face, even if parts of it are occluded or degraded.

It is worth noting that training such a hybrid model well requires a well-curated dataset which covers a wide variety of face variations and real-life scenarios. For this, we add to the training pipeline institutional datasets consisting of facial images of enrolled students and publicly available benchmark facial image datasets such as VGGFace2 and LFW. These datasets are preprocessed, including face detection, alignment, and normalization and aiming to maintain consistent input quality. We also apply different data augmentation strategies—random rotations, lighting changes and synthetic occlusions to simulate appearance variation and varying environmental conditions to help the network generalize across different situations.

The hybrid model is trained in a supervised manner of and it learns how to produce discriminative facial embeddings that are efficient in representing identit-specific characteristics of an individual. We are seeking to minimize the distance between embeddings of the same individual (intra-class) while maximizing the separation from other's embeddings (inter-class). To achieve this, the triplet loss function is used, where triplets are created such that the three elements are paired as (anchor image, positive image [same identity as anchor], negative image [different identity]). This loss makes sure that the embedding of a real user is always close to his historic representations compare to others fake. These embedded joint optimization, along with the respective advantages of CNNs and Vision Transformers in the hybrid architecture, render a capable and reliable real-time Identify verification system for online examination in the presence of the COVID-19 pandemic at the time of the writing of the research.

The hybrid facial recognition module is integrated into the general multi-factor authentication architecture through micro-services paradigm. In this architecture, every level of authentication (e.g. password checking, OTP verification and facial recognition) is a separate service in and of itself. This modular architecture permits each level to function independently, so that it may be scaled, updated or replaced easily without any need to compromise other system components operation. Such an architecture has clear modularity, maintainability, and extensibility advantages, as well as strong high availability and error recoverability guarantees by isolating potential failure points.

In addition, this design enables the system administrator to specify and control different levels of authentication severity depending upon contextual criteria. For instance, the administrator can onboard or apply facial recognition module dynamically just for high-risk exams, critical assignments, or whenever some form of abnormal or suspect user behavior is identified during exam a session. This situational responsiveness allows security to be graduated as necessary, balancing the ability to interact with the system with maximum protection. The proposed system scales well and supports resilience in security from the perspective of the changing need of online examination environments, benefiting from microservices and dynamic configuration.

Performance-wise, the hybrid CNN-ViT model clearly outperforms the CNN or LSTM models in spreading activation. Performance measures including accuracy, precision, recall, F1-score, and true positive rate (TPR), false acceptance rate (FAR), and false rejection rate (FRR), show that the proposed system outperforms the traditional methods in terms of the authentication accuracy and false positive and negative thresholds. Receiver Operating Characteristic (ROC) curve and Area under the Curve (AUC) analysis also confirm the discriminative capacity of the mixed model.

The impact of this research is far-reaching and is not limited to online exams. This proposed system reduces efforts on the part of avatars and improves security measures and trustworthiness of remote assessments to prevent the fraudulent participants by using the state of art AI technologies in the authentication process. This is achievement directly supports educational institutions in protecting academic integrity and also reduces reliance on a large amount of manual proctoring with heavy use of resources and susceptibility to human error.

In addition, the modular and scalable nature of the solution ensures that it can be easily adapted for other significant applications where secured identity verification is an absolute necessity. Possible follow-ups could be having remote access to sensitive information systems secured, allowing for trustworthy e-voting and enhancing identity proofing in e-gov and public services applications. By providing a flexible, AI-enabled multi-factor authentication model, this study provides a strong basis for the implementation of robust and trustworthy digital trust systems that can be effectively adapted to the security requirements of different sectors in a more interconnected world.

4.1 Hybrid model

The hybrid architecture is a thoughtful amalgamation of the best aspects of CNNs and Vision Transformers (ViTs) and acts as a good choice to build a hybridized strong and precise model for sequence dependent classification tasks which fits well to identity verification within online examination systems. CNNs are known to be very powerful in obtaining fine-grained local spatial features and textures from the input visual data, and such capability is important to represent a face accurately. On the other hand, Vision Transformers are good at modelling long-range dependencies and holistic global contextual correlations using self-attention in image patches.

Combining both of these architectures in one joint model, the hybrid model builds on the detailed local feature extraction power of CNNs and the wide, context-driven representative learning strength of ViTs. This combined behavior allows the system to produce rich, discriminative embedding that are both spatially precise and contextually-aware. Thus, in this case the hybrid system performs better in addressing the sequence data (e.g., continuous video or a multimodal facial input sequence) needed for a robust, real-time user authentication. This makes the architecture particularly useful for dynamic and high-security applications such as online proctoring, where regular, accurate, and reliable identity verification is essential to the integrity of the examination process.

Overall, the proposed approach is structured in a systematic manner with highly modular components which are coherent to provide a robust and reliable facial-based user authentication. The architecture initiates by utilizing Convolutional Neural Network (CNN) layers to capture fine-grained local facial spatial features of the input facial images. We then segment the processed feature maps by the patch embedding module into patches of fixed size that will be input to the transformer stage next.

Finally, the embedded patches are processed by several Vision Transformer (ViT) encoder blocks, which are designed to capture long-term dependencies and global context among the patches via hierarchical multi-head selfattention and feed-forward layers. This allows the model to learn holistic and semantically meaningful representations of the face which are not restricted to local patterns.

Then a MLP head on the top of network performs the final classification for Identity as the embedding get feeded through so that the inputs are classified for being an authorized user or not. Each of these architectural features is mathematically formulated with exact mathematical expressions, which can give us theoretical motivations about why local and global feature learning can be combined as a pipeline.

The overall sequential work-flow and the data flow of model has been visually shown in Figure 1 of the thesis to provide an insight on how the modules correspond with one another to provide an efficient AI-based, multi-factor authentication solution designed for secure online examination domains.

4.1.2 NN Layers for Local Feature Extraction

In the first part of the hybrid architecture, low-level and mid-level features are extracted from the input sequence (video frames or sequential images). We use the CNN layers, which are known to capture well the spatial patterns (e.g., edges, textures, facial landmarks) since contributions due to such local resources have thermodynamic interpretations. CNN receives a sequence of image as input and performs a convolution as defined in Equation (1):

$$X \in R^{B*L*D} \quad (1)$$

$$X_{conv1} = ReLU(X * W_1 * b_1) \quad (2)$$

$$W_1 = R^{F_1 * K_1 * D} \quad (3)$$

$$X_1 = R^{B_1 * L_1 * F} \quad (4)$$

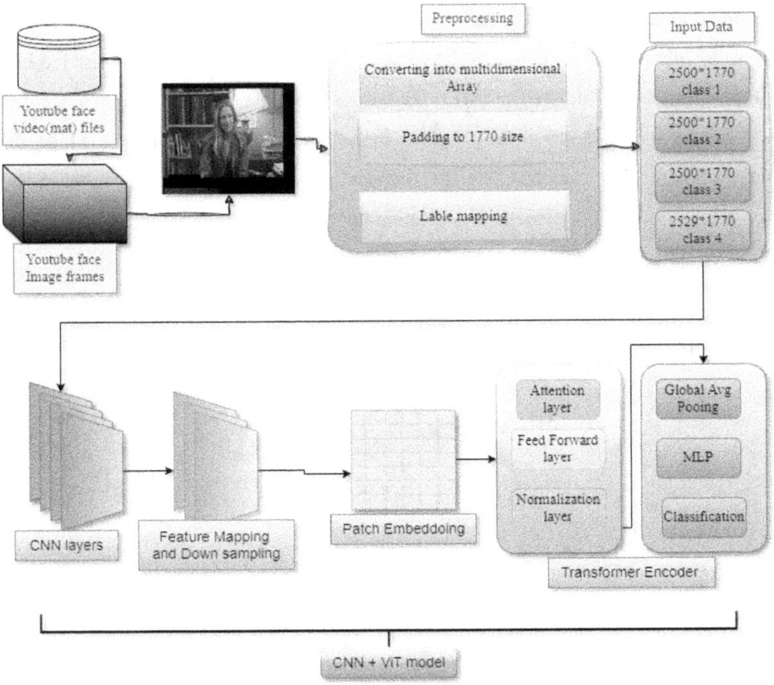

Figure 4.1 proposed hybrid model

The diagram demonstrates a hybrid deep-learning architecture that joints up a Vision Transformer (ViT) together with Convolutional Neural Networks (CNN) to perform facial recognition or classification with video data from the YouTube Face Database. The process begins with raw. mat video file that is decomposed to facial sequences by sampling frames. These frames are preprocessed by first converting them into a multidimensional array, padding to same length 1770 and mapping with the respective class labels. The prepared input data is passed through CNN layers (class 1 to class 4 are used as the example in the case of the input data classified into classes), where spatial features are extracted, and down-sampling is performed to decrease the dimensions and maintain the vital information.

After feature extraction, the output is pacified and projected to embedding's, that is termed as patch embedding, and serve for the transformer encoder. The patch wise information is processed by a Vision Transformer encoder, which is composed of an attention module to capture global patch-to-patch interactions, a feed forward layer for non-linear transformation, and a normalization layer to enhance the training stability. Then the encoded representations are fed into a global average pooling layer, followed by MLP layer, and final classification layer to predict the output class. The proposed CNN + ViT hybrid model, namely T-OC, fully exploits the advantages of these two architectures: the CNNs for the local visual patterns and the Transformers for the global context information, which is very suitable for face authentication and identity recognition in the real-time video data.

$$X_{pool1(B*\frac{L^1}{2}*F_1)} = Max\_Pool(X_{conv1}) \quad (5)$$

$$X_{conv2(B*L^{11}*F_2)} = ReLU\left(X_{pool1} * W_{2(F_2*K_1*F_1)} * b_2\right) \quad (6)$$

$$X_{pool2\left(B*\frac{L^{11}}{2}*F_2\right)} = Max_{Pool(X_{conv2})} \quad (7)$$

$$X_{embedd\left(B*\frac{L^{11}}{2}*1770\right)} = CONV1D\left(X_{pool2}, Filter = E, K_S = 1\right) \quad (8)$$

$$Q = X_{embedd\left(B*\frac{L^{11}}{2}*1770\right)} W_Q \quad (9)$$

$$K = X_{embedd\left(B*\frac{L^{11}}{2}*1770\right)} W_K \quad (10)$$

$$V = X_{embedd\left(B*\frac{L^{11}}{2}*1770\right)} W_V \quad (11)$$

4.1.3 CNN Layers for Local Feature Extraction

The first stage of the proposed hybrid architecture adopts CNNs for learning local, low-level, and intermediate-level features of input sequences. Such sequences can be a set of video frames or temporally resolved images, which are frequently utilized in applications like facial expression recognition; video action recognition, and identity verification. CNNs are well-known for their adaptability in capturing spatial hierarchies and detecting visual patterns such as edges, lines, textures, and complex structures. Such a feature makes them well suited for modelling repeated local patterns in sequential or spatio-temporal data.

In this layer, the input is fed through a convolution block which is trained and tailored to learn and refine fine-grained spatial cues. We start by a convolutive layer that works with 32 filters, which slide checking over the inputs to identify the relevant patterns of the local regions in them. The output of this convolutional operation is activated (element-wise operation with a non-linear activation function - normally Relu) which brings non-linearity into the network and allows the model to learn more complex data relationships. In order to facilitate the learning when training the model, batch normalization is placed after the activation function. This normalization operation normalizes the activations, alleviates internal covariate shifts, and facilitates faster and more stable convergence in training.

A dropout layer is used to enhance the generalization capability and reduce the risk of overfitting of the model. Dropout is a technique for training the network by randomly deactivating a certain percent of neurons in a network during each training iteration, preventing the network becoming too dependent on particular neurons. This will push the model to learn redundant paths for feature detection, which can help increase robustness/performance on unseen data.

Max-pooling is applied after dropout. Like max-pooling, this pooling layer reduces the dimensionality of the feature maps, only preserving the most prominent activations in a particular region of the map. In this way, it retains more essential spatial information and filters out less crucial spatial structures. This layer not only serves to highlight important patterns in the data, but also serves to make the next layers less computationally intensive.

The dimension reduction done by max-pooling also serves in decreasing the size of parameters in the model, hence making the model less likely to overfit the training data. It makes the representations easier to learn, because the network learns to ignore the meaningless distinctions within the input. What's more, pooling leverages translation invariance, or: the more an example's (novel) feature is located equally anywhere in the frame, the better the network will be able to grasp it.

Together, dropout and max-pooling play a strong regularization and compression role in the CNN architecture. Though dropout helps to make the model to learn general features by suppressing co-adaptation of neurons, max-pooling makes sure only the most important spatial features pass to the next layers. This synergy contributes to a more concise, time-efficient and generalizable model.

The generated feature maps from the first convolutional block are passed into the second convolutional block with 64 filters twice the size of that of the first block. Larger number of filters increases the ability of the network to learn complex and abstract features from the input data. At this point the model starts to learn mid-level features such as partial object shapes, facial parts like eyes or mouth or repeating motion elements in video sequences.

The second convolutional layer further extracts hierarchical features using 64 different kernels on the input feature maps. These kernels allow the model to understand the deeper structures and semantics of the input, thereby representing a richer visual content. Similar to the first block, a conv layer follows the convolution operation and ReLU activation for non-linearity to enrich the learning capability of the model.

Next, a second max pooling layer is performed again to condense the smaller features and reduce the spatial dimensionality. This operation is designed to remove parts of lossy information since only the most significant activations are kept and the others are discarded by the operation, efficiently preserving the computational complexity and decreasing the number of parameters. This deeper block of convolution, activation and pooling generates a dense, informative and concise description of the image.

The resulting visual representation, which now encodes more abstract and meaningful patterns, becomes the strong base for the subsequent part of the architecture — the Vision Transformer (ViT). Through the input of this processed representation into the ViT, the model could start to encode the global relationships in the whole image or frame sequence, naturally making better predictions at the new statement.

4.1.4 Patch Embedding Layer

Then there it comes a CNN component which extracts and compresses big spatial features from the input, and the generated output needs to be reshaped to fit in for the input requests of Vision Transformer (ViT). Unlike CNNs, which work on spatial hierarchies, Transformers are explicit about working on sequential data—a technique first implemented in applications such as natural language processing. Hence, in order to fill this architectural void, the 2D spatial feature maps formed by CNN are sliced into smaller equal size patches.

These patches are then flattened and reshaped into 1D-vectors and the spatial grid is thus converted to sequential representation. This operation allows the Vision Transformer to reason about image data in the same manner it would about word sequences in a sentence. Every patch is treated as a "token" in the sequence, so that the self-attention procedure can be applied over all patches. This "conversion" is very important, because it enables the Transformer to look at long-range relationships in 2D, between image-a-priory distant places, which are intuitively far spaced in the input image, but contextually close together.

The patch-based representation preserves the structure of image while matching the structure of the Transformer. Therefore, the model is able to make use of both local spatial features the CNNs can capture and the global context awareness of the self-attention layers in the Vision Transformer. This fusion is the key strength of the hybrid CNN-ViT architecture which serves as a strong baseline for tasks like image classification, face recognition, or action recognition.

The patches extracted from the CNN's output are then flattened (being flattened) into 1D vectors, retaining spatial information of each localized region. This flattening converts 2D shape of patches into a linear sequence so that it can be operated further in Vision Transformer (ViT) pipeline. After being flattened, these vectors are each passed through a trainable linear projection layer.

This layer projects vectors into a fixed-sized embedding space, thus standardizing the representation of each patch, regardless of its local extent.

This linear projection w as done to obtain a set of uniform and dense representations of the patches that could be efficiently handled by the transformer block. These are equivalent to word embedding in NLP, and are used as the input tokens of the transformer encoder. By parameterizing these transformations, the model learns to make sure that each patch contains a meaningful and comparable description of the corresponding spatial image region. This embedding is necessary for the self-attention mechanism to work effectively, so that the transformer can compare relationships and interactions between every patch in the same feature space. Besides the linear patch vector projection, positional embedding are used to retain spatial relationships in visual inputs for VG-T. Once transformed into a 1D sequence for the transformer operation, the spatial information of relative positions may be lost. To compensate for this, the original location of each patch in the image is encoded by adding a distinct position embedding to each patch vector.

Such positional embedding are trainable parameters that provide the model with explicit information about where the patches are located in space. And thanks to this added positional information, the Vision Transformer can retain knowledge of how each patch is spatially related to the others — something crucial for tasks that depend on the arrangement and layout of visual elements, such as object detection or facial recognition. Without position embeddings, the transfer would view an input as a flat sequence of tokens that have no intrinsic structure/order that might destroy spatial awareness. This might severely affect the model's visual understanding. It is why we need to add the positional embeddings to make sure the model well aggregates the local features from CNN and their global contexts.

The patch embedding layer is crucial for connecting the local feature extraction capability of CNNs and the global context modelling capability of transformers. It serves as a transposition layer, to transpose dispersed CNN features into sequential format, which also fit for transformer processing. The layer dissect the feature maps into small fixed-size patches, then embed each of them into a consistent vector space, thus preserving important local information while still allowing for sequential interpretation.

This transformation enables our model to interpret complex spatial information as an ordered sequence of tokens, in a similar way to how arbitrary transformers process input sentence words. Every embedded patch preserves the visuomotor appearance of its associated region which means no important spatial information is wasted. The embedding step further normalizes the input format and the transformer can be readily applied for visual input with arbitrary input resolution or shape.

Moreover, by combining patch embeddings with positional embedding's the special information of the patches is retained, this helps the model to not only know what a certain patch means, but also where it belongs to in the image. This kind of spatial-awareness is crucial for identifying global patterns, structures, or dynamics that thread together otherwise distinct locales.

The patch embedding layer fuses CNNs with transformers such that it facilitates an effective transition from local perception to global reasoning. It makes sure that transformer gets clean importance-rich representations to make better and contextually relevant decisions as they contain feature level detail and spatial position embeddings. This bridging mechanism is key to the success of the hybrid architecture on tasks requiring both knowledge and local accuracy in global patterns.

4.2 Vision Transformer Encoder

After obtaining the patch embeddings, they are fed through the Vision Transformer (ViT) encoder, which is achieved by exploiting global context and long-range dependencies of the input sequence. The ViT encoder is comprised of a sequence of modules that are applied to work iteratively and monotonically on all patches in the sequence.

The central component in an encoder layer is the Multi-Head Self-Attention (MHSA). This component enables the model to pay attention to various parts of the input sequence concurrently, and thus learn the relations between patches, regardless of the spatial distance between them. Utilizing multiple attention heads, the encoder is capable to identify a variety of patterns and interactions, we teach its representational capacity.

After the MHSA, each layer contains a Feed-Forward Network (FFN) that applies non-linear operations and another transformation to the attended features to make them more expressive. Within this framework, these feed-forward layers aid in learning complicated, hierarchical and non-linear features and add the depth of comprehension of the model.

Each encoder layer also includes layer normalization both before and after each attention and feed-forward blocks to ensure training stability and convergence. In addition, dropout layers are applied on the encoder to overcome the problem of overfitting and the model's generalization to unknown data.

Together, these parts allow the Vision Transformer to learn from high level semantically rich representations by relying on image-wide reasoning in a sequential manner. This global g-attention mechanism is particularly informative and indeed an asset of the ViT encoder for tasks that require access to a large receptive window in order to have a holistic interpretation of visual data. The transformer architecture is defined by the self-attention mechanism as its key component. It enables the model to focus on the most informative components of the input sequence by computing attention scores between all pair-wise combinations of patch embeddings. This mechanism enables the model to evaluate how strongly one patch should interact with another, irrespective of their spatial separation in the image or sequence.

It should also be noted that while CNNs has a weak stand on local relationships and tend to capture the nearby relationships, the self-attention mechanism provides a global view. It makes the transformer able to understand and capture translated and/or displaced distances between distant regions, which is a very important asset when it comes to global-context-enabled tasks. For instance, the model can learn motion cues by correlating over time (from multiple frames in video sequences). In facial recognition, it can identify symmetric parts by examining features on the other side of the face.

Furthermore, this mechanism permits the model to learn complex dependencies among objects or elements separated in space and time. In this way, the transformer learns to capture high-level patterns including scene composition, object co-occurrence, and structure regularities that are key to robust visual recognition.

To sum up, the self-attention mechanism provides the transformer the capacity to learn global, long distance dependencies that would be hard for the standard convolutional methods to capture. "which allows the model to understand the input data in a more comprehensive and holistic manner, thus greatly improving the performance of the model on complex visual tasks."

In order to improve its generalization power to learn different patterns and relations across the data, the transformer model uses several attention heads called Multi-Head Self-Attention (MHSA). Rather than depending on a monolithic attention, the input is divided, and multiple parallel attention heads operate independently. Each head attends to a different subspace in representation space, enabling the model to establish a wide range of dependencies and interactions at the same time. For example, one attention head may concentrate on localized texture patterns, while the other might capture long-range spatial relations or structural alignment. It is this parallel processing that helps the transformer to learn more nuanced and more globalized representations than what may be learned by a single attention head.

The output of each attention head is then concatenated to create a combined representation. This merged output is followed by a linear projection layer, which further fused it and projected it back to the original embedding dimension. This is motivated by the fact that the information extracted from different attention heads and the nonlinear transformation effects should be fused into a unified feature representation.

Subsequently, the output goes through the feed-forward network (FFN) where learned features are further processed with non-linearity and depth. This multi-headed structure greatly enhances the model's expressive ability to comprehend both detailed and global interrelations in visual data. Following each attention block of the transformer encoder, there are dropout and layer normalization for better training stability and model generalization. Dropout does so by stochastically deactivating some of the neurons during training so that the model cannot rely on specific connections. This stochastic regularization pressure helps the network learn to extract general and robust features. The similar scale of output is en-sured by the layer normalization. It offers the benefits by rescaling the activations, leading a more stable training dynamics, faster convergence and better performance.

In addition, residual connections are added around both the self-attention and feed-forward sub-layers. These skip connections can let the original input jump over certain layers and get added to the output directly, which is beneficial for gradients back propagation. It is particularly crucial in deep architectures as it alleviates the vanishing gradient problem and enables better training of deeper models. After the sequence of patch embeddings have rolled through the entire transformer encoder stack, the output is passed through Global Average Pooling (GAP). This pooling operation down-samples the sequence to which a single, fixed-sized vector that is the mean of embeddings of all patches. GAP allows local features (extracted by the CNN and early attention layers) as well as global context (modeled by self-attention process) to be combined into one representation.

The resulting vector is concise but informative about the characteristics of the input image or sequence. It is the end high-level feature representation that is fed to the final classification layer for prediction. We contend that a judicious combination of advanced attention architectures, normalization methods and pooling strategies has yielded a powerful and efficient hybrid model to address a variety of complex visual tasks.

4.3. Multi-Layer Perceptron (MLP) for Classification

The last part — classification head of the hybrid CNN-Transformer model is an MLP. This stage is responsible for understanding the deep, high-level feature vector produced by the vision transformer and mapping it to a set of output class probabilities. These probabilities are associated with certain labelling's such as identity, emotion, or finals in a specific application of the model.

The MLP is implemented as a dense network that have two densely connected layers. A Rectified Linear Unit (ReLU) is applied at the output of each layer. ReLU adds non-linearity to the model, and this non-linearity is needed when it comes to learning about higher-dimensional space from the layers prior. Without this non-linearity the model would be able to learn only linear mappings and they are usually not enough in the majority of classification problems.

The compact feature vector is fed into its former layer, and the first dense layer accepts this as input. This vector contains local features (from the CNN layers) and global dependencies (from the transformer layers). The second dense layer applies a linear transformation and ReLU to start to distinguish data points that could be assigned to different classes. The non-linear activation allows the network to explore more complex partitions of input space making the classifier more expressive.

The output from the first dense layer then goes through a second dense layer, which also applies ReLU activation. Such added transformation is more likely to enhance the ability of a model to refine its learned decision boundaries and to separate contact points arising from the small perturbation in input features. The widths and depths of these layers are usually decided according to the complexity of the dataset and the classification task. Dropout could also be used between the dense layers to avoid overfitting. Dropout randomly deactivates a portion of neurons during training, making the model learn redundant and general pattern instead of the training data. The overall effect is a more resilient and general classifier.

In the MLP, the last output layer is generally a softmax activation (for multi-class classification) or a sigmoid (for binary classification). This layer generates the class scores of the image through turning the raw outputs into normalized probabilities. The predicted label is the class with the maximum probability.

During training, the model optimizes a classification loss—e.g., categorical cross-entropy—computed as the discrepancy between the predicted probabilities and the true ground-truth labels. Through back propagation and optimization, the MLP learns the best possible weights to reduce this error.

In general, it can be said that the MLP is the decision-making part of the hybrid framework. It connects the low-level, abstract features learned deeper in the network with the requirement to generate interpretable and clear predictions. Due to the non-linear transformation, the MLP can model very complex decision boundaries, and is thus suitable to solve difficult tasks such as face recognition, emotion classification and visual object categorization.

In order to improve the generalization capability of the model as well as to prevent overfitting, dropout layers are inserted between each fully connected layer of the MLP. During training, dropout stochastically turns off a fraction of neurons in each iteration. This reduces overextending the network on set of paths and features by forcing the network to learn more widespread and repetitive representations. Therefore, the model becomes more robust and generalizes better to unseen data, by learning to generalize patterns rather than memorize the training examples.

Dropout is a kind of regularization, which forces the network to explore a wider range of solutions. By training on different mini-ensembles of the active neurons at each iteration, the model effectively emulates a number of different networks, which greatly improves its generalization behavior. Such stochastic resampling during training offers some degree of resilience to noisy samples and can be beneficial into preventing the overfitting to small datasets or very deep models.

After the dropout-augmented transformations, the last layer of the MLP is a multi-class softmax output layer. The softmax function takes the raw outputs from the output dense layer — typically referred to as logits — and converts them to probability scores across all classes. As such, each output node gives a value between 0 and 1, and the sum of all of the outputs equals 1, yielding interpretability as class probabilities.

This probalistic capability has two main benefits: it allows us to take the most likely class simply by picking the class with the highest probability, and it gives us confidence in the prediction, by comparing the probability with the rest, the model can weigh whether it's very certain of its decision. Such information can be critical for real-world decision making, such as when a system must be able to express a certain degree of confidence in a prediction, e.g. for facial recognition or medical diagnosis.

To sum up, the adoption of dropout in the MLP layers not only promotes the generalization and robustness of the model, but also guarantees the accurate and interpretable classification outputs by the softmax layer. When used together, they provide a strong combination that combines deep feature learning with accurate decision-making helping in boosting overall performance of Hybrid CNN Transformer architecture.

4.4 Hybrid Model: CNN + Vision Transformer Integration

The hybrid architecture enjoys the best of both worlds between CNNs and ViTs, leading to an effective model to tackle sophisticated sequence-based classification problems with better accuracy and generalization performance. CNNs are designed to extract local features and to realize spatial hierarchies of input data which have proved to be particularly effective in the early stages of visual processing. Their convolutional layers aims to find edges, textures, or fine details which are consistent in various positions in images. However the receptive field of CNNs are limited and cannot cover long range dependencies or contextual relationships which exist over long spatial or temporal distances.

The Vision Transformers, however, are designed to capture global dependencies using self-attention. Transformers, aside from CNNs, have all-to-all connectivity, and evaluate every pair-wise relation between input elements, at the level of the input sequence, where they are capable of learning complex structures or interactions occurring between remote areas or frames. Global context modeling is essential for tasks relying on relational reasoning (e.g., motion between video frames, structural symmetry between facial images, relations between distant objects within a scene).

While transformers are very express and flexible, they often need large datasets to achieve their best performance. This is because of the absence of inductive biases— like translation invariance and locality—which are built into CNNs. Pure transformer models may therefore have difficulty generalizing and learning efficiently from small or noisy training datasets.

The hybrid model combines the advantages of both architectures by consolidating CNNs and Vision Transformers. The CNN backbone extracts strong local features and compresses the input into a compact representation which is fed to the transformer. The transformer component extends this representation to incorporate higher-order dependencies and global structures. This kind of synergy encourages the architecture to simultaneously focus on the fine-grained feature extraction and the broad contextual comprehension for the sequence-based problem, e.g., facial recognition, emotion classification, and action recognition.

More generally, the hybrid architecture combines the data efficient and local specialization of CNNs and the contextual richness and long range modelling capabilities of transformers, and demonstrates improved performance and adaptability across a breadth of visual recognition tasks.

By combining CNNs with ViTs, the hybrid mod-el harvests the complementary benets of two architectures. CNN layers that live in the host serve as an effective low data hard front-end responsible for extracting low level and mid-level visual descriptors (textures, edges and localized patterns). This new building-block is much more lightweight than the traditional blocks and can learn discriminant features even with limited training samples, which makes it more suitable for the early-stage processing.

Following the CNN, which extracts valuable spatial features from the input, information is converted and fed into the Vision Transformer. In this section, the local information can be regarded as special cases of the global information, which can be used to capture high-level abstractions, and also more capable of modelling long-distance dependencies over input sequence. The transformer is particularly effective in finding distant relations in the sequence, e.g. motion continuity through frames or symmetrical facial features, leading to a better grasp of challenging spatial and temporal relationships.

This end-to-end design can ensure the free flow of information, and can naturally integrate the advantage of CNNs in local pattern extraction and the advantage of transformers in global modelling. Therefore, the hybrid model is data efficient and computationally efficient to learn rich and diverse representations from the raw video input. As a result, it is especially appropriate for computationally demanding computer vision challenges such as recognizing identities from video, where specific facial features need to be tracked continuously through time; emotion recognition, which requires recognition of delicate expressions; and activity classification, which depends upon consistent time-sensitive information over video frames.

While the complementation of CNNs and ViTs enables the model to adapt to both the detail and the context, which makes our framework achieve highly accurate and generally applicable results for different kinds of vision-based sequence classification problems.

4.5 Model training

The hybrid CNN-ViT model was trained over 18 epochs releasing a greater degree of hyperparameters and with an intense focus on tuning them to gain higher classification accuracy and generalization. The number of output classes, which specified the structure of the final classification layer; the embedding dimension, which essentially controlled the size of the patch representations fed to the Vision Transformer; the number of attention heads, which played an important role on the model's capacity to capture diverse relationships within the data and the feed-forward network hidden size in the ViT, which influenced how well the model could learn complex transformations.

All of them are chosen so that the trained models have just the necessary expressiveness and avoid over-fitting and overly large networks, while being large enough to generalize sufficiently well. This tuning was essential for the overall performance of the architecture, and especially for personalizing the model to the particularities of the input data and the task.

Optimization The model applied the Adam [35] which is known as one of popular gradient descent descent algorithms having the property of an adaptive learning rate, fast convergence and robustness of training deep architecture. Adam is a robust optimization algorithm because it combines the best properties of AdaGrad and RMSProp. It works well for a variety of designs and can handle large- or sparse-scale gradients and non-stationary objective functions.

Semi-supervised training employed sparse categorical cross-entropy loss which is suitable for multi-class classification problems with integer labels of true distribution rather than one-hot encoded labels. Its computational efficiency and the ease of interpretation for dense and sparse signals make it more suitable to predict discrete class labels from a fixed set of categories.

Taken together, the training methodology—optimizer, loss definition, and hyperparameter tuning—were designed to encourage stable generalization learning provided by NSA. These choices led to higher efficiency of the model in learning from complex input sequences and ensured its robustness across varied classification tasks, including identity recognition, facial expression analysis, and action recognition.

In the training step, the hybrid CNN-ViT model was trained on a specific training set and then its performance was assessed on a separate validation split. This approach enabled monitoring of the model's learning dynamics in real time and enabled tracking of early signs of overfitting, when the model is too closely adapted to the training data, or underfitting, when it cannot capture meaningful structures in the input. Tracking validation accuracy and loss during the training, provided valuable feedback about the generalization capability of the model and helped to correct the training parameters as necessary.

The use of validation data meant that any adjustments or tuning made during training were informed by an independent measure of performance and not solely by the training data. This preserved the integrity of the training and testing process and protected against the possibility of creating a model that fits only training samples well.

After training was done, the model received extensive testing on a separate test-set to make sure that it had not seen that section of data before. This test stage was crucial to the determination of the actual generalization power of the model and provide an estimate as close as possible of the performance we could expect in deployment. The trained model was tested on this new data to verify if the learned features and decision boundaries were reusable.

Strong classification performance on final test results indicated that the hybrid architecture could extract meaningful, discriminative features that generalised well beyond the training distribution. This improvement further demonstrated that our model design and training paradigm is valid and suitable for practical sequence-based vision classification tasks like identity labeling, emotion recognition and activity classification in real-world scenarios.

The learning curves shown in Figure 2 provide a clear indication of the learner's performance growth in the process of training. More specifically, the chart on the left demonstrates the trends of precision, during 18 epochs for the training and testing sets. As we can see, the training accuracy increased with every epoch, finally achieving a very high value of around 98.8%, which suggested that the model was good at learning patterns from the training set.

Meanwhile, the testing accuracy similarly increased smoothly and following the development of the training accuracy, albeit consistently below, which is usual in well-generalize models. This strong overlap of the two learning curves indicates that the model was not only memorizing the training data, but was also learning features that generalised well to unseen samples.

Most importantly we don't have a wide gap between the 2 curves meaning that we are not overfitting which is the typical issue in deep learning where the mode works really well on training data but not okay on validation or test data. On the contrary, The almost parallel and closely associated behaviors of the curves suggest strong generalization and healthy learning.

This consistent level of performance on these datasets is an evidence on the validity of the hybrid CNN-ViT model, the training approach, and the hyperparameter selection. It shows that the model was able to preserve effective and consistent classification performance for all phases of evaluation proving its generalizability in practical tasks that include complex visual and sequential data.

As another view beside the accuracy trends, in the right graph of Figure 2 shows the loss curves of the training and testing data, providing further understanding of the learning dynamics of the proposed hybrid model. In the initial passes of training, you can see a strong decline in loss, reflecting that the model very rapidly started to pick up on and adapt to the structure of the input data. Such a dramatic drop is typical of strong early learning, in which the model shifts its weights aggressively to minimize the prediction error. As the training proceeded the loss values slowly started to converge to a point where further learning had less and less effect. This plateau in the loss curve is very strong evidence that the model was actually converging and not oscillating or diverging after having converged, something that can happen in poorly-tuned and / or over-parameterized models.

At 18 epochs, the final training loss was about 0.005 - a miniscule value that means the model is very confident and accurate when it comes to predicting the training data. At the same time, the testing loss leveled slightly higher than at 0.010 when compared to the training loss. This small margin between training and validation loss is a strong indicator for the model having high ability to generalize. The small gap between the two loss curves suggests that the model was not overfitted; it had in fact learned the meaningful features in the training data and kept them when presented with unseen data. Overfitting usually appears as the training and the testing losses diverging (widening)—which we particularly see nothing of here.

Furthermore, the similar assimilation rate and down sampling rate is consistent with the other, which indicates the utilization of regularization methods in our model (e.g., dropout layers) and careful hyper parameter-setting. The model's consistent low error and high predictive accuracy in different datasets demonstrates its stability and reproducibility.

It is clear that the good classification accuracy, low and balanced loss values and smooth learning curves are very strong evidence of the robustness of the proposed CNN-ViT hybrid architecture. It demonstrates that the model can not only learn complex visual and sequential patterns, but can also leverage them in order to perform various downstream tasks, e.g., identity recognition, emotion recognition, or action recognition.

In conclusion, as can be seen here on the loss curves and accuracy trends, which convincingly give demonstrations to us that the model is capable of learning high-quality patterns with the best generalization, and it is possible to be widely studied for the practical deployment in the scenario of visual recognition tasks to obtain the both precision and the reliable.

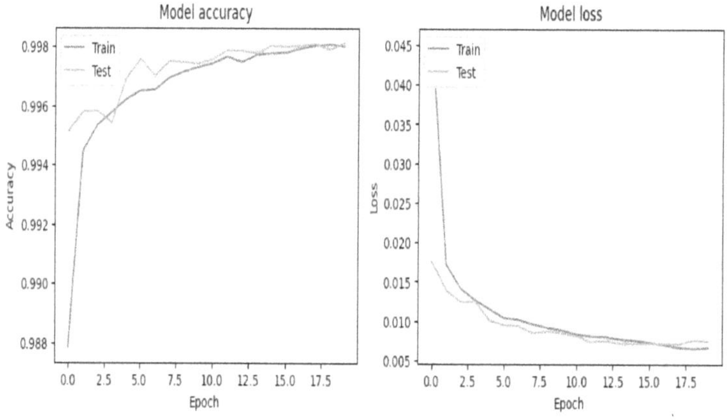

Figure 4.2 training and validation curves of hybrid model

Figure 4.2 demonstrates the training and validation curves of the trained hybrid CNN-ViT model for 18 epochs. The left side plot shows the model's accuracy (i.e. the percentage of times the predictions are correct) on both the training and testing data. A jump in accuracy is observed within a few initial epochs, which indicates that the model can quickly extract useful features. Training accuracy eventually hits 0.998 and the test accuracy tails closely behind at about 0.9975. The proximity of the two curves demonstrates that the model generalized well while there is no indication of overtting, which is a common problem in deep learning models.

On the right, conclusively, the loss curves support this observation. Both training and testing loss decrease dramatically at the beginning of training, which indicates efficient learning of the intrinsic data structure. As training proceeds, values of the loss start to plateau, with both the final training loss reaching around 0.005 and the testing loss at 0.006. The fact that the difference is small tells you that the model is well-regularized and the performance is stable with respect to unseen data.

In general, the hybrid model is robust and efficient as a result of the two high and close performance metrics, low loss, and smooth convergence of both curves. These findings confirm the model's ability to classify efficiently for identity and emotion recognition, and reliability in practice.

4.6 Over view

This chapter provides a detail study of design, development, and performance analysis of a Hybrid CNN-Vision Transformer (ViT) based MFA system to improve the security of online examination system. By combining the benefits of local feature extraction by Convolutional Neural Networks and global context modelling by Vision Transformers, a system capable of robust facial recognition under tough, practical conditions is presented.

The hybrid architecture provides the ability of modelling of both fine-grained facial details and long-range dependencies and thereby enhancing the identification accuracy of people. This facial recognition module is part of a multifactor framework where it is used along with traditional authentication factors (i.e., username password credentials) and One-Time Passwords (OTPs) to create a multi-layered approach to user authentication.

This AI-based form of authentication represents a significant advancement over traditional methods and is capable of providing heightened security as well as more intelligent and responsive user experiences. Converging biometric with token-based checking injects several layers of checks, without compromising usability -- an especially important consideration in online learning settings where securing users' identity matters.

The model is explicitly designed to mitigate the growing need for veracious, scalable, and human-in-the-loop-based examination systems that can function robustly across multi modal devices and illumination or background conditions. It also decreases the possibility of impersonation, unauthorized access and so on through the most usual forms of identity fraud in on line testing environments.

The rest of the chapter will dive deeper into the full development process. This consists of: a thorough description of the proposed methodology, the hybrid system architecture, the dataset alignment, the training strategy, the validation strategy, and finally, the performance metrics that were used to evaluate the accuracy and robustness of the model.

Also, a set of experiments is offered in the chapter to see the superiority of this hybrid CNN-ViT model with the traditional and most recent recognition systems. The performance is evaluated including the recognition accuracy, processing time, scalability and anti-spoofing.

Additionally, a comparative study is obtained to compare the proposed method with other models, which demonstrates that the hybrid model achieves good performances in both academic data sets and staffed productions. Through these detailed examinations, the chapter refers the proposed MFA system as a very promising implementation towards securing and maintaining integrity of online examination and a milestone in relying cutting-edge biometric-based authentication technologies for digital academic platforms.

CHAPTER 5

Block-chain-Integrated Multi-Factor Authentication System for Enhanced Security and Decentralized Integrity in Online Examination Platforms

5.1 Introduction

Development education technology is one of the fastest growing sector in education, revolutionizing traditional teaching and assessment practices. Among these developments, the online examination system has emerged as a major facilitator for remote learning and assessment. While these platforms have many advantages such as flexibility, scalability across hundreds of thousands of diverse students, and lower administrative costs.

However, moving to digital examination mode brings various new security problems. This includes the hurdle of maintaining the process of the exam to be fair and authentic. In contrast to offline exams, where students can be inspected personally, online exams are sensitive to cheating from proxies, sharing identities, or other malevolent behaviors, that may degrade the fairness of the assessment.

One of the most problematic issue is unauthorized access, where people who are not the test candidates try to take the test instead of them. Nothing is more ridiculous than a system in which people can cheat their way through it and still come out with a certificate, because it makes a mockery of qualifications, and this involves reputation of schools that have distance learning in place. Lack of physical invigilation provides students with a broad way of malpractice, like assuming false identities or sharing login credentials.

In order to maintain the integrity of academic tests it is important to deploy methods that are capable of securely verifying the test-taking student's identity at all times during the examination process. Sound authentication guarantees that only legitimate test-takers can access and take the examination, thus maintaining the integrity and reliability of the outcome.

With online learning gaining ground, the imperative to fix these security holes is not just a technical need but a philosophical one as well for establishing credible, transparent, and equitable educational landscapes. This security gap is continually being addressed by hybrid solutions, which integrate traditional authentication methods with new, innovative technologies like biometric identification and AI-powered authentication to rebuild trust in remote testing.

In order to address the security and integrity issues of Internet based examination system, the author proposes a Multi-Factor Artificial Intelligence (AI) Based User Authentication System. The main purpose of such a system is to offer a secure, smart and strong authentication system so that just rightful candidates come in the digital exam room. Using the strength of multiple layers of authentication, the solution is intended to help mitigate and thwart security risks starting at relatively low-risk identity mismatches to higher-risk impersonations and fraud.

Classic login approaches, e.g. Single Sign-On (SSO), are often used as a comfortable and common access control dealing with centralized user authentication but generally are not suited for high risk actions like academic assessments. SSO is susceptible to password deprecation, password sharing, and also third part parties having access and as such are not fully suitable as the sole security practice for exams. Acknowledge these shortcomings, the proposed solution consists of several layers of authentication which brings in a more solid approach.

The elements of this multi-factor system are as follows:

1. **Username and Password Verification**: Standard username and password pairs to start user verification. Metadata delivery is typical based on the Metadata Host configuration. This is the barrier between anyone trying to break in.
2. **OTP Verification** – To enhance the second step of the process, a one-time token (OTP) is dispatched to user's registered email or mobile. The upshot, it eliminates static credential abuse and provides real-time proof that the client is authorized to access the account.
3. **AI Based Facial Recognition Layer** – The face feature layer is provided by a deep learning-based facial recognition model, which is based on a hybrid CNN-ViT structure. This verifies that the individual that is trying to log into the test platform is the actual candidate who has registered with CFA Institute and is very secure for identity authentication.
4. **Livens Detection and Spoof Prevention** – Advanced computer vision technologies incorporated to identify spoofing attacks, including those using static images or pre-record

videos. This is an important step in ensuring that a real-time, live presence is being recorded and is being verified.

5. **Continuous Monitoring (Optional Extension)** – In extended or high-stake exam environments, self-paced re-authentication can be initiated with periodic face re-verification to make sure that the same user is being active during the entire examination.

Taken together, these ingredients create a rich and robust authentication structure that can lead to a significant reduction in impersonation, password sharing, and harmful actions. Artificial intelligence at the core of the system increases security and trustworthiness (added to the current demand to smart and scalable solutions in modern digital educational ecosystems).

Utilizing AI, including deep CNN's, for facial recognition, artificially introduces a potent and intelligent third layer into the mix of multi-factor authentication. It adds a strong security layer on top of the traditional ones, for facial features are unique and they cannot be easily transferred/shared/duplicated as password or OTP does. Therefore, the face recognition can offer a reliable and dynamic approach to identify the student during online exams.

But there is something special about this layer: it indeed incorporates deep learning methodology as the model is being trained with a triplet loss. This advanced learning method augments the capability of the model to discriminate the authentic user and the imposer in the presence of minor difference in facial information. Triplet loss achieves this by training the network to minimize the distance of centroids/codes of a true pair (anchor and positive) and maximizing the distances of a true pair, and one false pair (anchor and a negative pair) by a margin. This results in discriminative facial embedding that allow for accurate and invariant recognition.

This technique can be utilized on live video streams and the technique can facilitate real-time facial verification that is required to prevent impersonation while a candidate is taking the exam. Compared with static image matching, live-stream analysis also helps to ensure that the user is physically present and engaged, making it harder for someone to trick the system with a printed photo or pre-recorded video.

This AI-based facial recognition layer, will not only contribute to ensuring the integrity and trustworthiness of the examination, but also provides a more simple and passive verification process for test-takers. It reduces the repetition of manual entry and continuously protects against the possibility of identity theft. To sum up, the triplet loss-based CNN facial recognition technology raises the system's overall performance in providing secure, intelligent, and tamper-proof identification, which is a vital prerequisite for the next-gen online exam security platforms.

5.2 proposed Block chain-Integrated Multi-Factor Authentication (BIMFA)

The traditional model poses problems that higher educational institutions face due to of the lack of systematically checking and verification solutions for examinations in their network environments, which increases exam insecurity, unguaranteed integrity, and general distrust in online examination. 2.1 The proposed B IMFA system presents a comprehensive solution for the challenges of security, integrity and trust in online examination environments. By combining state-of-the-art deep learning methods, behavior biometrics, and decentralized block chain technology, BIMFA introduces a multi-faceted system intended to authenticate users with high accuracy, stop identity theft, and protect sensitive information via distributed storage.

To this end BIMFA is designed to be modular in construction, comprising of three core elements that together deliver a strong and smart authentication process:

Hybrid CNN-ViT Model for Face Recognition: The system features an AI-enabled biometric layer at its front-end, powered by a hybrid of Convolutional Neural Network and Vision Transformer (CNN-ViT) for real-time facial recognition with 99.7% accuracy. This model can well represent both local facial characteristics and global spatial patterns, so that it may identify accurately even under complex environment. Learned with a method like triplet loss, the model aims to learn discriminative feature embedding, and then prevent fakes accept and rejections.

Verification of behavioral biometrics: In addition to the facial recognition module, behavioral biometrics is included in the system to ensure the authenticity of the user according to the patterns of interaction. It may contain keystroke dynamics, mouse movement, or gaze dynamics in the course of exam session. These behavioural traits are hard to emulate and still providing an ongoing, passive authentication, providing extra confidence for the system.

Recording and Management of Records on Block chain: For transparency and tamper resistance all the authentication events and user interaction logs are written to block chain based ledger. This distributed storage deterring censorship system ensures data integrity so as to provide a secure, audit-able, and tamper-proof way for records to be keep without fear of them being deleted or forged by any party (or parties) that are not authorized to do so. This adds a level of integrity to the system, which is especially important in high-stakes educational environments.

These three layers in combination create a very secure and scalable authentication infrastructure that can be suited to the demands of the contemporary online examination systems. The combination of AI and block chain does not only improve the accuracy and reliability of user authentication, it also scales with the general needs of data privacy, integrity, and transparency.

Through the use of this BIMFA framework, the academia may comfortably shift to research less examination systems while being reassured of the authenticity and integrity of the individuals appearing in the examination that they are supposed to be. The system constitutes an effective solution to the problems of traditional single-layer security models for online assessment, and highly promotes the upgrading, producing a new model of online assessment security for next generation.

A close-up look of the conceptual framework of BIMFA system is given by Figure 5.1 in which we present the interactive mechanism between BIMFA's AI-based models and block chain-integrated infrastructure. The architectural overview was made to demonstrate how it supports the use of a complete multi-factor authentication system, which combines 3 different types of validation categories they are knowledge based, possession based and biometric based factors.

The knowledge-based layer consists of common authentication factors such as user ID and password, which are considered the first factor. Although in use and popular, this method lacks security as it is lustful for theft or sharing. To improve security, the second layer brings in possession-based proofing in the form of OTP authentication. The OTP is sent to a registered email/mobile number ensuring the user has familiarity with at least one trusted device/channel during the time of login.

The next and most sophisticated layer has biometric-based authentication, which fuses facial recognition using hybrid CNN- ViT model with behavioural biometrics, like foot-tap dynamics or the patterns of mouse movement. These biometric characteristics are intrinsically and extremely difficult to duplicate and provide a very robust and dynamic mode of verifying identity.

When combined, these three layers create a multi-dimensional authentication pipeline which is not just dependent on what the user knows and has, but also who the user is. The system are also enhanced by the fact that block chain keeps a tamper-proof decentralized record of all authentication even though (line thirty three). Every verification is cryptographically logged for full transparency, accountability and immutability. Such an integrated approach significantly improves the system's capability to protect from impersonation, unauthorized usage, and types of digital malpractices and hence applicable to UOLP to preserve the integrity of on-line examination systems.

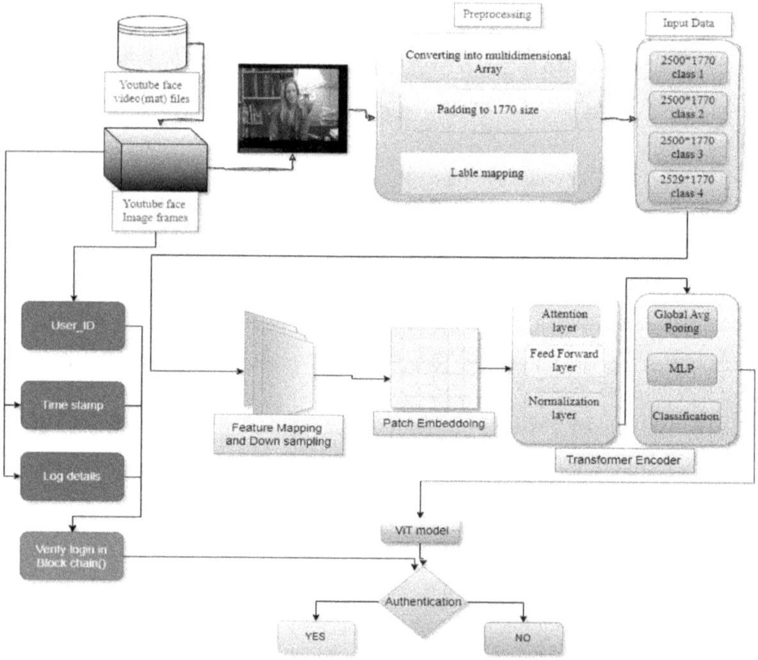

Figure 5.1 BIMFA system

The complete system architectural overview of the proposed BIMFA (Block chain-Integrated Multi-Factor Authentication) system integrating deep learning, biometric identification based authentication and block chain based secure and robust identity authentication in online examination systems is shown in Figure5.1.

The first step in the process is to ingest YouTube face videos in. mat format. In this way, these video inputs are decomposed into a set of image frames on which facial analysis can be performed. The pre-processing block starts and transforms the frames into a numpy array, the array is zero padded up to 1770 (which is the maximum number of samples of the usable input video) and the mapping from label names to classification indices is included. This input consists in sets of features labelled by a number of classes that are assumed to represent the different identities.

Concurrently, it will also take User ID, timestamp, and log—important metadata that is sent to the block chain component for later evidence-of-interaction. This way each login process is recorded and persisted in an immutable manner for accountability and auditing.

The image data is then forwarded through CNN blocks for local feature extraction, feature-weighted representation, and down sampling process to down sample the spatial dimension while maintaining essential information. The processed features then are partitioned into patches in patch embedding module to be used as the input to the transformer block.

In the Transformer Encoder, every embedded patch undergoes a series of operations of multi-head attention, feed-forward neural networks, and normalization layers. Such operations enable the model to capture and learn local and global image relationships. The output is then aggregated using global average pooling, followed by a MLP that connects to the classification block, which predicts the identity.

The prediction is generated by the ViT and is then verified in the authentication component. The forecast is checked against the block chain -- correlating user ID and log data and facial authenticity. In the event of successful authentication, the system responds with a "YES" response, allowing the student access to the exam. In any other case, it outputs a "NO", which means a wrong password was sent.

It's this structure that allows for a layered, tamper-proof and AI-enabled form of authentication. The fusion of the capabilities of deep learning in facial recognition, behavioral metadata, and decentralized block chain authentication makes the system highly secure, accurate, and transparent for online exams.

The facial recognition module lying at the heart of the proposed system is based on a hybrid deep learning architecture that combines the merits of CNNs with Vision Transformers (ViTs). It enables the model to capture local details and global context from facial image accurately, which is critical for robust identity authentication in practical applications.

At the early stages, the CNNs are adopted to obtain low-level and mid-level spatial features from input face images. These comprise fine-grained details such as skin texture, edge profiles, facial geometry, and local shading configurations. Convolutional filters of the CNN layers convolute the input image in a manner of pattern detectors scanning throughout the image. These filters are learned to be responsive to salient visual indicators and enable the network make richly discriminated facial features encoding.

By exploiting the spatial hierarchies of CNNs, they are especially well-equipped to focus on specific facial features, in spite of variations such as pose, expression, background, and illumination. Pooling and down sampling layers come after the convolutions attenuating spatial information and preserving essential information. It not only reduces computation overhead, but also helps the model generalize to various facial appearances.

These spatial feature embedding provide the basis for further processing in the Vision Transformer part of the model. The output of CNN (after CNN process) is divided into several equally sized patches before fed into the ViT model, and then are reshaped and projected into the high-dimensional space. This conversion allows the ViT to process the input image as sequential input like text in natural language-based (NLP) tasks.

The hybrid architecture enables the CNN part to capture fine-resolution spatial cues, while the ViT part captures the long-range dependencies and context cues across the facial regions. Results show that the proposed approach greatly improves the performance of recognition, even with incomplete and non-ideal conditions associated to the image.

Because of their handling of noisy environments and varying lighting conditions (e.g. rotated head, low visibility), CNNs are the ideal candidate to be used as a front-end in the recognition pipeline. These properties guarantee that the system does not work based on follow-up experiments for stability and reliability will be available for real-time examination circumstances where face angle variations are unavoidable.

In particular, the dependency of the facial recognition module on CNNs in local analysis help to ensure a robust as well as a competent feature extraction module. When added to ViTs for global modelling, the system receives the better of the two architectural worlds, and the resultant model is accurate, scalable, and secure when behaviour of the facial identity changes in different environmental and user-specific aspects.

5.2.1 CNN Feature Extraction

CNNs are especially good at detecting and learning local visual features, such as edges, curves, contours and textures. In the proposed facial recognition system a bank of CNNs is utilized to process each arriving video frame or single face image through a set of well—defined convolutional layers. Each of these layers use a collection of filters that slide across the input image, looking for distinct patterns in small areas of the input.

These filters allows to produce feature maps that are sensitive to different parts of the facial image—like the eyes, the nose, the lips, and skin textures. With stacked convolutions, the model learns increasingly abstract, complex face features that enable it to discern between individuals with subtlety.

The non-linear activation functions ReLU are used behind every single convolutions to enhance the learning capability of the network and keep the gradients stable. These activations serve to largely introduce non-linearity into the model, without which the model will not be able to model non-linear relationships that simple linear models cannot. In addition batch normalization layers are used to normalize the outputs from each layer which speeds up training and helps the network to maintain stability during training updates.

Pooling layers (such as max-pooling operations) are applied after the convolutional layers. These blocks perform down sampling of the feature map, essentially reducing its dimensionality but still keeping most powerful activations. This not only reduces computational overhead but also makes the resulting representations to become compact and robust as the most discriminative facial features are preserved.

This local feature extraction process makes the model relatively robust to non-face-related appearance change of the eyes, mouth, nose, cheeks and the jaw, such as Illumination, Pose and others. The CNN approach has been designed to be robust against light changes, head tilts, partial occlusions (e.g. glasses or hand), and expressions. The block also serves as a strong and robust baseline for the following Vision Transformer module to contextuate these local patterns globally. Taken together, the CNN-based processing pipeline ensures that important identity-specific features are encoded early in the recognition task, and therefore the system can predict reliably and confidently in a large variety of real-world situations.

Concurrently to the CNNs that compute local image features, Vision Transformers (ViTs) consider the global structure and dependencies inside the facial image, helping to equip the model with additional capacity. Instead of directly feeding the whole image as input, ViTs first divide the input image into fixed-size patches, and then these patches are flattened into 1D feature vectors. These vectors encode visually-relevant information extracted from individual regions of the face and act as tokens in a sequence-like input.

To maintain the spatial arrangement of the face, i.e., positions of the eyes, nose and mouth, positional encodings are appended to each patch embedding. The positional information will guide the model in knowing where every patch was originally in the image - this is an essential task since transformers, unlike CNNs, don't have any inherent knowledge of spatial locations.

Once we have embedded and positionally encoded 1 the patch vectors, we simply run them through the self-attention mechanism of the Vision Transformer. This helps the model understand inter-patch relationships and the relevance of different face areas. For instance, if one eye is partially blocked, the transformer may use the visible eye and other nearby regions to infer symmetrical or identity related characteristics. This capability to capture long-range dependencies provides a unique advantage to ViTs—by modelling global wide context that CNNs might overlook given their limited receptive field.

13 Global reasoning can be especially useful in practical scenarios where facial images may be distorted, occluded, in abnormal poses, or under non-uniform lighting. The ViT allows for robustness when considering the whole configuration of the face, and not only some local patterns. And the dual benefits can be added to the facial recognition module by hybridizing CNN and ViT outputs. CNNs capture very discriminative local features which are very sensitive to local patterns & textures, while ViTs represent a large view, and capture geometric relationships across entire face. This combination contributes a more complete and robust facial representation that can enhance recognition performance and robustness even with varying conditions.

Overall, the CNN-ViT hybrid architecture enables the model to integrate local and global information well and yields excellent performance for facial recognition in (dynamic and less-controlled) examination settings.

$$F_{(i,j,k)} = \sigma\left(\sum_{p=1}^{P}\sum_{q=1}^{Q}\sum_{r=1}^{R} I_{i+p,j+q,r} \cdot K_{p,q,r,k} + b_k\right) \quad (1)$$

$$Att_{(Q,K,V)} = softmax\left(\frac{QK^T}{\sqrt{d_k}}\right)V \quad (2)$$

$$f_u = cancat\big(eq(1), eq(2)\big) \quad (3)$$

The features from these two pathways are concatenated to form a fused feature vector after the facial image has been processed by the CNN and ViT modules. This fusion operation combines localized patterns encoded by the CNN (e.g., skin textures, facial contours, edge details) with global dependencies and contextual relationships modelled by the ViT (e.g., symmetry, spatial position, cross-region coherence).

The concatenated feature vector is a rich and high-dimensional representation of facial identity that is able to encode both detailed and global information (attributes). This dense representation is then passed through a fully connected (dense) layer with further transformation, taking it from

100 to 50 dimensions. The final output is to classify the facial input to a set of predefined identity classes by a classification function, which is often realized using a softmax activation function.

Such a hybrid classification scheme can largely enhance the accuracy of the recognition system. With the advantageous combination of CNN and ViT-based architectures, the model is more robust and robust in adverse imaging conditions.

Besides the accuracy, this approach has better robustness against spoofing and the resilience to adversarial attacks such as those created by deep fake technologies. Since minute textures cannot be well recovered and consistent cross-region facial relationships are not well mimicked in deepfakes, the dual-level analysis of this hybrid model can hardly be fooled. The system thus stand as a strong technique offering secure identity verification and can be very useful in sensitive applications such as online exam, accesses control, or digital authentication.

In addition to facial authentication, BIMFA flexes its security perimeter to a second biometric modality based on behavioral biometrics. This middleware module provides an RF (Radio Frequency) Based system of single user authentication using Keystroke dynamics analysis, which is one of the most current biometric verification techniques relying on the way individuals interact and respond as a characteristic of who these individuals are. Behavioral biometrics, on the other hand, do not use physical properties but the method with which a user interacts with devices.

Keystroke dynamics consists in measuring some characteristics of the keis, as the durations of they are pressed, the delay between the key down and the next key down, etc. Everybody has a unique keypad dance, and choreography is influenced by muscle memory, cognitive process and hand-eye co-ordination. They provide a human behavior signature that is very hard to forge, even if an imposter is using your same keyboard or device.

By continuously modelling these patterns during the authentication and testing process, the system is able to perform in real-time identity verification. For example if unexpected or inconsistent behavior like very fast key presses, abrupt timing of keys, or different pressure patterns are detected in the users typing behavior these might indicate the invaders or some proxy. Let the system then alert or initiate re-authentication protocol to mitigate the threat.

This passive but ongoing verification serves as a silent sentinel during the examination period. This is beneficial since unlike facial recognition, which can be applied just in one checkpoint, behavioral biometric tracking runs throughout the session, and you have ongoing comfort the user who authenticated at one point as the same as the one who is presenting now. This is especially important in the case of identity theft, that is, cheating or session theft in which an examinee might try to trade places with someone else after signing in.In particular, behavioral biometrics is non-invasive and does not need any additional device, thus easy to integrate the existing digital exam infrastructures. They work silently behind the scenes, leaving your user experience unaffected, while improving both security and usability.

By stacking behavioral biometrics on top of facial recognition along with factors such as credentials and OTPs, the BIMFA system creates a multiple-defense security shield. This two-level protection doesn't just impede unauthorized users, but actively checks for any irregularities in high-stakes tests. This ensures that the whole examination process is legitimate and fair.

Transparency, accountability and data integrity are core values of B2B, B2C, C2B and C2C within the BIMFA system, doing so with the use of the block chain. Unlike usual centralized structures in which distributed might have data visited or changed, block chain provides a tamper-resistant ledger to keep all of the authentication process reliably in distributed, immutable data formats. This way every attempt to login (valid/invalid) is logged and audit enabled.

The user ID, timestamp, verification result, etc., are the key information of each entry in the block chain. These are encapsulated in individual transactions, cryptographically linked and appended to the block chain in order. "Each transaction is also recorded in a distributed form in a "block" of other transactions that, when added together, comprise the record of the ledger or database." This arrangement prevents any record from being changed or deleted with Intelligent out approval from the entire network, preventing tampering by a single entity that administers the network. The latter process is managed by smart contracts in the BIMFA system. These are scripts that run automatically on the block chain to authenticate and record an authentication. Whenever a user asks to be authenticated, password, OTP, facial recognition, behavior biometric, the smart contract evaluates the far-end verification outcome and stamps the result to block chain in real time. This guarantees fairness and consistency across every transaction, eliminating the possibility of human bias and minimizing errors or omissions.

Smart contracts also provide for real-time auditability such that authorised parties (eg exam regulators or system administrators) can audit a complete, time stamped list of user authentications within the system. Being cryptographically signed, the block chain ledger confirms the data validity and non-repudiation; that is, no user or system administrator can dispute or tamper with any authentication attempt that has been registered.

Furthermore, the block chain ledger is not openly accessible, and is accessible under those role-based permissions-registered access policies: that is, the general public (non-stakeholders) cannot directly view/query whatever data is entered, protected the privacy aspect while keeping it auditable. This has the effect of making the (conceptual) block chain layer not just a log file but an active bodyguard of trust, forcing all identity verifications to be recorded, uniform, and tamper-proof. Through the use of block chain, it adds weight to its mission of creating a trustworthy, verifiable, and transparent authentication system, something particularly important in sensitive areas, and especially in those, as with online exams, where the credibility of a user's identities has crucial influence over the integrity of the entire system.

```
Algorithm:
    Start:
    block chain = initialize_block chain()
    smart_contract = deploy_smart_contract()
    user_id = get_user_id()
    timestamp = get_current_timestamp()
    status = authenticate_user(user_id)
    event_record = (user_id, timestamp, status)
    signed_record = sign(event_record, private_key)
    add_log_to_block chain(smart_contract, signed_record)
    block chain.store(signed_record)
    log_id = get_log_id_from_event(event_record)
```

```
        is_valid = verify_log_in_block chain(smart_contract, log_id,
    public_key)
end:
```

The use of the cryptographic signing, which is in combination with a PKI (Public and Private Key Infrastructure), is critical for providing the authenticity and provenance of each authentication record in the BIMFA system. Each transaction (successful login, failed biometric challenge, OTP mismatch) is cryptographically signed with the originating entity's (e.g., the system's authentication engine's) private key. This signature is such that it can be verified using the corresponding public key, and it assures whoever receives the data that the data has not been modified, and that it has actually originated from a trusted source.

This process strengthens the block chain's place as an immutable reliable audit trail, recording a chronological and secure report of all authentication statuses. Every event recorded in the block chain – the users' ID, the time of access, the type of authentication that was carried out, the output – is pearled and permanently written in the block chain, so that no unauthorized changes can be made to it.

We observe that this cryptographically based foundation skill fully serves system administrators, exam proctors, and academic auditors by providing a clear and trustworthy mechanism for retrospective auditing. In the cases of subsequent examination actions or identity disputes, block chain provides instant check-and-verify function for interested parties to verify immediate and full status of access attempt on the block chain to find out whether its being accurate or not. As all entries are signed and time-stamped, they provide irrefutable evidence of what took place at examination and avoid any conflict or reliance on oral evidence.

This could be particularly beneficial when it comes to claims of impersonation, mid-session substitutions and other false access, where evidence needed to make a fair judgment can be difficult to come by. In the end, digital signature with block chain makes the authentication process accountable, tamper proof and legally defensible, boosting confidence in the integrity of the holistic online examination system.

A new paradigm of secure facial recognition, behavior-based authentication, and block chain system via smart contract for the future is introduced by BIMFA system. These three elements are combined under a probabilistic model of decision making to estimate the probability of a valid access attempt. Each of these constituent modules -- whether physiological, behavioral, or cryptographic -- adds its own confidence score from its local analysis. These scores are fused to obtain the final score, which dictates if access request is accepted rejected.

The multiple modality probabilistic approach adds a level of adaptability to the system. If one component yields uncertain or borderline results, for example, a face that is partially hidden from the camera, or an outlier in typing rhythm, the system does not crash entirely. It rather combines the advantage of the other modules to a well-informed and self-consciously access decision. This redundancy-in-ballast has advantages for reliability, for robustness, and resistance to spoofing or evasion, meanwhile keeping false negatives or inconveniencing users low.

The BIMFA system is implemented with an organized and automatic pipeline for energy efficiency and scalability. The process starts by setting up the block chain network and deploying smart contracts which enable autonomous agents to validate events and log data. These agreements are how we determine what is permitted when recording auth attempts and ensures a standard process is followed, not an ad-hoc inconsistent one. Upon a user starting the process for authentication, the first step is to verify the knowledge-based credentials (e.g., username and password) and the possession-based token (e.g., OTP received over SMS or email). These legacy layers are the first gatekeepers.

At the same time, the system triggers facial recognition module that utilizes a mixed CNN–ViT model to authenticate the identity of the user based on the user's face with reference to the stored biometric templates. At the same time, the behavioral biometrics module examines keystroke dynamics or other such interaction patterns to measure the user's behavioral coherence.

The knowledge, possession, and biometric layers are respectively combined, and processed in the probabilistic fusion engine, which compares the aggregated data and calculates the final access decision. If the sum of confidence scores is above a predefined threshold, then access is provided. [Otherwise the system does not let the passenger enter and can ask to be checked again or to trigger a security alert]. Through the integration of AI-biometric, block chain, and a probabilistic logic engine, the BIMFA system provides a balanced, secure, and user-centric authentication form—perfect for use-cases with high-stakes such as online exams or secure digital platforms.

Once the authentication is complete, the BIMFA will create a structured event record which contains pertinent session information. That would be the user ID, the exact time of the auth attempt, and the outcome (e.g., authentication succeed or access not granted). This receipt is a documented, authenticated summary of the authentication exchange.

The event record is then signed with the system's private key (based on public key infrastructure [PKI]) to provide both integrity and authenticity of the data. This cryptographic fingerprint tells the recipient that the message is genuine and has not been tampered with. Any tampering with or unauthorized modification of the record would render the signature invalid instantly, providing a clear indication that the record is not trustworthy.

Once signed, the document is sent to block chain using a smart contract. Smart contract can see record, verifies it automatically, checks the signature, append transaction to the de-centralised distributed ledger. That way, the record is immutable, transparent, and tamper-resistant, and available to only authorized parties who have the rights to access them.

Upon successful submission to the block chain, the system gives back a unique log identifier, as a reference to the particular authentication event. This identifier can be used by an administrator, auditor or proctor of the examination, to track, audit, or follow the results of that session.

Using the corresponding public key, any party can independently validate the authenticity of the event log by accessing block chain, and affirm its source and integrity without dependence on centralized bodies. This step introduces a rigorous element of transparency, non-repudiation and trust into the process of authentication, making the system more trustworthy - particularly when it comes to sensitive situations such as academic exams or secure system access.

The decentralized nature of the BIMFA system contributes to a more transparent and trusted system. Distinct from conventional databases vulnerable to fraud, downtime, or a single point of failure, BIMFA uses block chain distributed ledger to guarantee authentication records are almost instantaneous to access, verifiable and tamper-proof by those authorized. Such a high-level of decentralization enables system operators, auditors, and test takers alike to verify abstract user identity and access history, for compliance with academic honesty standards and regulatory criteria.

It could be concluded that the BIMFA (Block-Chain Integrated Multi-Factor Authentication) ecological system delivers an integrated, secure and scalable authentication service, which is also designed for UEPs. By combining hybrid deep learning-powered face recognition, behavioral biometry analysis and block chain-based decentralized logging, the system effectively counteracts weaknesses of conventional means of authentication.

Its multi-tiered verification approach strengthens the platform's resistance to various forms of threats, such as password breach, deep fake-based spoofing, command identity fraud and in-session identity swap. The method isn't based on any single means of verification but rather fuses an entire suite of authentication signals in an intuitive probabilistic decision model for a perfect balance of accuracy and robustness.

In addition, block chain technology is leveraged to indisputably record every validation event in an immutable manner, creating an indelible and auditable path of accurate, reliable information that affected parties can utilize for dispute resolution and compliance audits. This serves to strengthen the integrity of digital evaluations, and encourages a higher level of personal accountability and trust within the user base.

With the increasing trend towards digital learning and remote assessment, the BIMFA platform becomes the modern solution that will change the status quo for integrity, security and transparency in online education. The approach is valid for current and future problems, offering a future-proof authentication model that takes in account the evolution of security threats by guaranteeing users a seamless use.

5.2.2 Vision Transformer for Global Context

Although very effective at learning local visual features (e.g., edges, textures, small spatial patterns) on facial images, for instance, CNNs have an inherent limitation of the receptive field to model global dependencies across facial regions. That is to say, the face is mainly structured by the global and local information that have different spatial distribution and it is hard for CNNs to represent them sufficiently when the cues are far away from each other, or the input is not good, such as pose variation, partial occlusion, or misalignment.

To overcome this limitation, here we bring in Vision Transformers (ViTs) as a complementary tool. ViTs use self-attention to capture correlation between all pairs of pixels in an image, allowing the network to capture global context. It is simple to feed-forward the input image to a CNN to obtain rich spatial feature maps, which are then cut into uniform non-overlapping patches. Each patch is then flattened into a 1D array of size V and projected down toC, resulting in a sequence of embedding for the tokenized image.

These token embedding are subsequently enriched with positional encodings that denote the position of each patch in the input spatial grid. The transformer block's self-attention mechanism is utilized to automatically infer the importance of patches in relation to every other patches in the sequence to build relationships between parts of the face in a structured and long-range dependent manner.

This procedure greatly increases the recognition capabilities of the system (i.e., to recognize a face even in conditions of small expression changes, lighting variations, pose distortions or occlusions). Through the combination of CNN's local feature extraction and ViT's global reasoning, the hybrid model not only can capture both local spatial context and global relationships with much balanced performance, but also shows higher robustness and reliability, especially for high-stakes identity verification applications, e.g., online examination authentication, border control, or secure system access.

Feature Fusion

There are two representatives in the hybrid-based method of face recognition and the feature fusion has great significance in the combination of the strengths between CNNs and Vision Transformers (ViTs). CNNs provide the finer-grained local features—describing textures, edges, and micro-expressions, and ViTs add a global contextual embedding, accounting for spatial relationships and the geometrical relations of the whole face.This combination results in two separate feature sets that are concatenated in the unified vector representation, thus combining the precision at localization level of CNNs with the holistic understanding of ViTs. This fusion is usually carried out at the level of embedding, e.g. via external concatenation, attention weighted sum or bilinear pooling. The high-dimensional vector is with span of both spatial detail and global structure, so it is well designed for discriminative facial representation.

This concatenated feature vector is then passed to a dense layer (fully connected) which ends in a softmax activation which provides class probabilities that map to the saved identitions in the system. At deployment or at runtime trial, the system acquires a facial input, computes its fused embedding and compares it with the pre-enrolled embeddings present in the database by measuring the similarity between them, for example cosine similarity, Euclidean distance.

By aggregating local and global cues, the fusion mechanism remarkably boosts the accuracy, decreases the false positive, and increases resilience to spoofing attacks with printedphotos, masks or deep fakes. Being a dual-view representation it enables the model to carry out discriminative identity verification in presence of adverse conditions such as changes in lighting, occlusions, or pose. To sum up, the feature fusion schema turns the output of CNN and ViT networks into a strong, holistic, facial signature, which makes the hybrid model such a reliable instant identity classification and verification with high accuracy — perfectly suited for critical cases in the form of online examination security, e-KYC systems, and access control authentication.

Behavioural Biometric Verification

The second layer in the BIMFA authentication, behavioral biometric authentication, improves reliability by maintaining values of what the user does and how he types (keystroke dynamics). Facial recognition is a great first step in authenticating the user, but it's an exactly-once process. Behavioral biometrics provide a continuous and passive mode of authentication guaranteeing that the authenticated user is the same throughout the session.

The keystroke dynamics are the pattern of how individuals type keyboard including key press duration, flight time between keys, typing speed, rhythm. These patterns are unique to each user and are hard to reproduce even if an attacker knows the user's credentials.

The system is always in the background of an online test or secure session listening to these typing patterns. The recorded patterns are then compared to a previously enrolled behavioral profile for the user. In case it detects that some aggressive changes are happening in the connection, it is possible to generate alerts in real-time, ask a re-authentication or even close the session to avoid a potential fraud.

This layer provides a critical layer of security to guard against threats like mid-session impersonation, proxy test-taking, and credentials sharing. Even if an individual will somehow bypass or spoof the facial recognition layer, their typing behaviour will be different from that of the legitimate user and the system will be able to suspect unauthorized access.

As a result, behavioral biometrics is a non-invasive, ongoing protection method that strengthens the security of who is allowed into or out of the system and all but guarantees that the person who originally started the session is the person who finishes it.

Data Capture and Feature Extraction

In the BIMFA system with behavioral biometric module, the KB-stroke patterns are being collected all the time when user is authenticating or being tested by the system. It includes fine-grained information such as the time that the keys are pressed (dwell time) and the time between successive key presses (flight time). These raw timing sequences are collected on the fly when the user is using the system. These may seem such trivial numbers, yet they tell the truth of heavily learned behavioral traits affected by a myriad of motor skills, muscle memory, hand-eye coordination, knowledge of the keyboard layout and even the user's posture. Their unique pattern of behaviour becomes their own, and with time are both enduring and individual — it is your cancer fingerprint."

After capturing the raw keystroke data, it is fed into the feature extraction process to convert timing sequences to a set of structured feature vectors. These metrics can be statistical in nature such as average press duration, standard deviation of flight times, timing priority between common pairs of keys and n-gram typing patterns. This step of transformation allows the system to normalize the input data for comparison and further analysis.

The obtained behavioral features are subsequently utilized to enroll or authenticate a new user profile or an existing user profile. As typing dynamics are considered something that is hard to consciously mimic this level of authentication is a strong mechanism to prevent a user for being impersonated by, even attackers who know the correct password or have a valid face image.

By monitoring keystroke dynamics patterns in real-time the identity verification is enhanced at login level, and a real-time monitoring of the behavior of the user taking the exam is kept along the entire examination to coherently verify that the same user keeps active the full exam time.

Modelling and Verification

The feature vectors derived from the keystroke data are then supplied to statistical or machine learning models as executed by the computer system for real-time comparison to the user's enrolled behavioral profile. Support Vector Machines (SVM), Multi-Layer Perceptrons (MLP), Random Forests, K-Nearest Neighbors (KNN), etc., are few such techniques generally used for modelling of biometric patterns. The model takes the incoming feature vector as input and generates a behavioral similarity score indicating the similarity of the user's current typing behavior compared with their enrolled profile.

The higher the similarity score is, the more the newly detected behavior is in accordance with the habits of the registered user, and therefore the user can also be verified and maintain the session. Conversely, the lower the score falls to a certain threshold indicates a large IBV and the system will consider it as a probable impersonation or unauthorized use. In such instances, the system may generate an alert, temporarily prevent access, or initiate a second level of authentication using facial re-authentication or proctor intervention.

Session-Focused Security

Unlike other conventional means of authenticating identity in the initiation phase, the keystroke dynamic method allows continuous authentication of the user as long as the interaction (e.g., an on-line examination) takes place. This active behavior surveillance ensures that the log-in user is the same user at the end of the working session.

This is important to identify signs of mid-session threats, like proxy testing or collusion, where someone else might attempt to take control of the session after the original login. As soon as an anomaly in the typing pattern is recognized by the system, it may be capable of issuing a real time an alert of an abnormality and also to take pre-emptive measures to ensure the session's integrity.

Through the profiling of behaviors and integration of continuous verification within the lifecycle of the session, the BIMFA system not only authenticates access, but also maintains identity assurance which is very much a cog in the wheel in high- risk scenarios such as online exams, secure communications or sensitive digital interactions.

Block chain-Based Audit Logging

In order to improve the transparency, the data integrity and the trustability, The BIMFA system includes a block chain audit logging function. This layer makes sure that all authentication things, the successful ones and the others – are recorded permanently and securely as a transaction on a permissioned block chain network. In this way, it removes the dependence to centralized databases which are open to tampering and creates an immutable, decentralized audit trail.

Distributed Ledger and Smart Contracts

Underpinning this logging mechanism is a shared log that maintains records of all the important steps of the authentication pipeline: the user's sign-in, OTP, facial recognition match, and the behavioral biometric scores. These events are then processed and recorded automatically via smart contracts a type of self-executing program stored on the block chain. These agreements ensure data is consistent, captured securely, and preserved from human error or manipulation.

After an authentication event is registered, it is added to the ledger permanently and cannot be revised or removed, ensuring the temporal integrity of the records. This unfalsifiable trail is important for post-scan validation allowing institutions to confirm in order and authenticity of ID checks.

Cryptographic Assurance

To provide authenticity and non-repudiation, each log in a block chain is digitally signed with the private key of the system. This signature cryptographically proves that the log comes from a trusted source and has not been altered. List any party with interest may verify the author of and the authenticity of the entry using its own public key.Furthermore, every log entry is time-stamped, providing a reference to the chronology of events. This is especially important for conflict management, such as reported impersonation or cheating, where parties involved are able to track actual authentication events which can be verified for authenticity using an irrefutable record about the time the authentication event did occur.

In sum, the block chain based audit logging solution is a cornerstone for trust, transparency, and accountability in the BIMFA system. It is a user interaction recording that is tamper-evident, an automated method of compliance (e.g., with academic or regulatory standards), and an independent verifiable way to ensure integrity in high-stakes digital environments like remote tests or secure digital on boarding.

5.3 Evaluation of the BIMFA

The proposed BIMFA system shows superior contribution in the advancement of the user authentication module for online examination systems, with focus on security and reliability. Central to the architecture of the system is a novel hybrid face recognition model, which takes the advantage of the Convolutional Neural Network (CNN) as well as Vision Transformer (ViTs) at the same time. This fusion enables the system to take advantage of CNNs' capability of extracting detailed local features, like textures and facial landmarks, while ViTs has a global view, which models long-range dependencies and spatial relations over the entire face.

Through combining the local and global representations of facial features the hybrid model effectively learns facial structures resulting in a strong ability in recognizing users even under challenging scenarios such as different illuminations, occlusions and subtle facial gestures. The ability of the model to focus on finding and recognizing subtle facial expressions and context-aware features is instrumental to reduce the false positive rates and counter impersonation attacks such as deep fakes and static photos.

That is the recognition rate that the system achieved and it's simply incredible, it's impressive," he adds. Testing the boundary Closer study of the data and recognition scores produced by the system left them confident that the authenticity system was robust, accurate and hard to deceive in real-world settings. So that the stage of initial identity verification is not only rapid, accurate, but based on very difficult to tamper or bypass, and provide good hardware support for the multi-level security of BIMFA.

This high level of trust is a prerequisite for the proper functioning of online exams where authenticating examinees is important to avoid cheating, impersonation and misusing the credential. So, when it comes to face based bio-metric module of BIMFA system, it becomes a reliable front line guard, as a support to the BIMFA system's mission to secure the education places by intelligent and adaptive authentication mechanism process.

In addition to the high-precision face recognition layer, the BIMFA system includes a module for behavioral biometric verification (BBV) based on keystroke dynamics, which further enhances a level of continuous and passive user verification. This part of the component aims to ensure that every episode of typing behavior observed in any user can observed as unique to that user, and includes features such as key press durations, flight times between keys, the rate of typing, and typing rhythm—all of which are also a part of who we are, not just how we type, and they change subtly overtime making it near impossible for even someone with your device, credentials, and password to mimic you while keystroke dynamical surveillance is in operation.

In order to model and validate such behavior of the entities, a Random Forest classifier is used, an effective ensemble learning technique known for its robustness and good over fitting resistance. This classifier processes extracted keystroke features and compares them to pre-enroll user profiles to establish user identity consistency in the session. The behavioral biometric module achieved 95.6% authentication accuracy, which demonstrates its capability to distinguish nominated participants from impostors with high confidentiality by the interaction patterns. The fact that this accuracy is achievable in a non-intrusive and dynamic verification setting is especially notable, since the user needs to take no extra action – he can user his device as usual. In so doing, this module serves to improve the systems mid-session threat detection capabilities, eg in the form of proxy test taking, unauthorised hand-overs or attacks driven by bots, by allowing for real-time monitoring of consistency of behaviour. If abberant, statistical keystroke behaviour is observed during the examination, the system may activate warning signals, add additional security checks or actions (dual authentication), or may immediately take action to protect the soundness and inviolability of the examination session. In short, keystroke based behavioural biometrics in BIMFA system add a necessary second layer of security. It does so by making the identity verification process secure not just during login, but also ongoing and adaptable, supporting an overarching objective of preserving exam security, integrity, and fairness in digital learning.

One of the other notable evolutions of the BIMFA philosophy is the use of block chain technology for secure, transparent and tamper-proof logging of all authentication operations. All events during the authentication, including login, validation of an OTP, face matching, behavioral biometrics result, are recorded as an immutable transaction on a permissioned block chain registery. This way, the entire lifecycle of authentication is in a time sequence and no other settings including logs be tampered or deleted. In validation (still system validation), we need do a lot of performance test for the block chain that it is used for checking the availability, stability, immutability and access control policy. No one will ask questions or view these result set, but authorized parties (say a administrator or auditor) can query and view these results, which further tells you that... 1) Your data is private 2) Your systems works effectively. By removing centralized logging risks, including altered logs, unauthorized changes and compromised log data, block chain becomes a 'trust anchor' to enhance fairness and make post-exam audit and dispute resolution easier to adjudicate.

Simultaneously, the classification performance of the BIMFA model was exhaustively measured under the same dataset, corresponding to four-class, expressions of different user profiles or authentication results, that is, legitimate users, pretenders, the failed logs, and also the anomaly. The model showed high class-based classification accuracy; precision, recall, and F1-score all consistently neared 0.98. Those measurements demonstrate that the system is not only effective in authorizing the access but also proficient in reducing the number of false positives and negatives, so that it can work soundly and stably in different authentication situations.

In combination, the utilization of block chain based logging and the strong multi-class classification performance firmly establish BIMFA as a complete and smart identification solution. Not only it guarantees the identity verification but it also has a clear and verifiable certification audit trail which is ideal for high-risk settings such as remote exams, digital on boarding and secure online platforms.

5.4 Overview

The BIMFA approach combines hybrid AI-driven facial recognition, continuous behavioral biometric verification, and decentralized logging via block chain into an unbreakable, single authentication framework. It's a distributed, what I call, multi-modal approach, where its CNN-ViT facial recognition strength is combined with the strength of CNN-ViT-based biometrics keystroke behavioral tracking, and it combines with the block chain strength, where it cannot be changed, and it's transparent.

By using two of these technologies together, BIMFA provides a tamper resistant, real-time, multi-factor authentication strategy tailored to the requirements of online examination system. By re-authenticating identity with each action and recording intractable logs of events, it helps prevent impersonation, proxy testing and unauthorized access by confirming only authorized users can both gain and maintain access. In so doing, BIMFA not only increases technology security, but also can better the establishment's credibility and the confidence of the users. The system enables access to fair, valid and secure assessments by overcoming limitations of conventional login methods and is scalable and easy to deploy in different types of digital learning environments. Combining BIMFA with remote and hybrid educational models is an important next step for secure, transparent, and trustful authentication in digital education ecosystems.

CHAPTER 6

DATA SET and Result Analysis

6.1. Data Set

The security and dependability of a biometric-based multi-factor authentication (MFA) system depend heavily on the quality and consistency of the dataset that is used to train its machine learning models. We used YouTube Faces Dataset for the proposed BIMFA system, a vast publicly available dataset containing facial images extracted from video and for various subjects. This database provides real-world facial expression variation, lighting variation, and orientation variation and is well-suited for training robust facial recognition systems in uncontrolled scenarios such as those we would be expected to encounter in online exams.

Acquisition and Extraction of Data

The YouTube Faces dataset was at first saved with a compressed file format (i.e., TAR file), which is a type of TAR archive, used by the TAR archiving tool to store multiple files and directories. The archival method has kept the hierarchy of the dataset intact, which is necessary in order to preserve the relationship between the facial descriptors and their corresponding subjects. A well-organized directory structure was found after TAR file extraction, in particular the descriptors_DB subdirectory. The directory had a bunch of files ended in. mat) file, one containing pre- calculated facial features described by different descriptors.

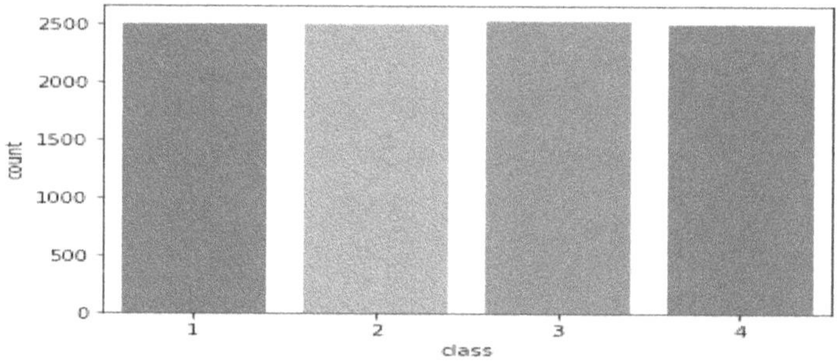

Figure: 6.1 Data distribution dynamics terms of four different classes

The bar chart in Figure 6.1 shows the distribution of the data in the four alternate classes in the training and evaluation dataset of the proposed authentication model. We can observe that the numbers of instances from different classes are quite balanced. This type of balance in class representation is essential in the supervised learning scenarios as it prevents the model from having a bias toward any one specific class. A balanced dataset makes sure that the classier has a same chance of learning the features related to the respectively category, which benefts for the generalization performance on all classes. The uniform distribution also helps in having fair evaluation metrics like precision, recall, f1-score for each class, which leads to more realistic and practical performance of the model. Finally, the well-balanced class distribution plays a key role to the strength and performance of the BIMFA authentication model.

Descriptor Types and Representation

Among the descriptors in the. mat were local Binary Patterns (LBP) and the Color Local Binary Patterns (CSLBP), known to be effective in texture-based face recognition. LBP describes the micro texture of facial areas by encoding the local structure of intensity images, while CSLBP augments this by incorporating the color information, providing better discrimination under different illuminations. Each. each mat file included one or more descriptors referring to the facial image or a frame of the video of a given subject. These files containing descriptor often had different shapes and structures, influenced by the number of features that were extracted for each sample. As such, it performed a cautious data traversal to discover and load all relevant. mat files systematically. A strong data loading system was used, allowing an iteration over the directory structure, determination of files with meaningful descriptor data, and extraction of these features, accounting for inconsistencies in their internal format.

Table 6.1: Extracted mat file and its embedding and padded vector with dimension 1*1770

	[[0.01204679 0.01204679 0.01204679 ... 0. 0. 0.][0. 0. 0. ... 0.33199912 0.23858432 0.2560116] [0.12223514 0.06413483 0.15045299 ... 0. 0. 0.] ...[0.23997515 0.33462936 0.32436687 ... 0. 0. 0.][0. 0.11393885 0.15260361 ... 0. 0. 0.][0.18658376 0.2147122 0.16525602 ... 0. 0. 0.]]

Table 6.2: different class and number of samples

Class Label	Count
1	2500
2	2500
3	2500
4	2529

Figure 6.2 An excerpt from the dataset

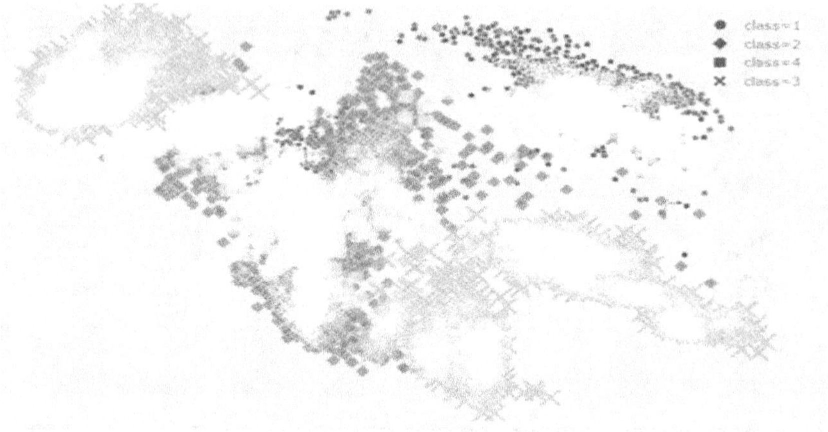

Figure 6.3 The scatter plot reflecting the visualization of data set consisting of four classes

In Figure 6.3 we have a scatter plot, showing the sample distribution and clustering among four different groups in the data set. Classes are all shown in separate marker types - class 1 as circles, class 2 as diamonds, class 3 as crosses and class 4 as squares—so you can distinguish between the categories. This plot demonstrates that the samples from each class are clustered together to varying degrees, however some degree of overlap at the boundaries is still present. This visual separation establishes that the feature extraction and dimension reduction processes employed in the pre-processing step have successfully projected high-dimensional data to lower dimension space without compromising class-wise separability. The overlapping portions indicate regions where classification may be difficult, which emphasizes the need for a robust model formulation for the purpose of accurate predictions. As a whole, the scatter plot gives us a nice peek at the underlying composition of the data, which also validates meaningful patterns that the model can exploit for multi-class classification.

Data Normalization: Padding and Trimming

The pre-processing of the responses in our case posed us with the problem of having the descriptor vectors of swirl slightly differing in dimension for different examples. To learn the hybrid model (CNN-ViT) uniformly, we need to make the feature vector shape to be constant.

When examining the descriptor vector lengths, the maximum dimensionality among all samples was 1770 dimensions. For any sample with a smaller number of features, zeros were appended to reach that dimensionality, and samples with more than 1770 features were truncated. This strategy allowed samples to have the same feature vector length, as expected, in "batch" processing and matrix arithmetic in deep learning libraries.

After pre-processing, the total number of samples was 10,025, with four different classes. Each sample was reduced to a common shape (1770,), and when stacked the complete data set consisted of a matrix of dimensions (10025, 1770).

Class Distribution and Balance

The problem was formulated as a four-class classification problem, corresponding to different users or authentication environments of the MFA system. The number of samples of these four classes are listed in Table 6.2;

It seems balanced, the only smaller imbalance is the class 4 with 29 more samples than the remaining. Figure 4 shows a graphical depiction of the class distribution in the dataset validating that the dataset is workable for training without the need of a heavy oversampling or under sampling technique.

For multi-class decision scenarios such as in a user authentication system, a balanced class distribution is also important, as a false acceptance or a false rejection in this context may lead to severe security consequences. The roughly balanced ratio of positive and negative samples of each class can prevent the classifier from being subjected to a biased training of the dominant class, thereby maintaining high performance in all authentication clusters.

Exploratory Data Analysis (EDA)

Prior to passing the data to the hybrid CNN-ViT model, we conducted an Exploratory Data Analysis (EDA) so as to better understand how the features and classes are related with one another. This entailed the visualization of high-dimensionality descriptor data by means of PCA.

PCA is a method for reducing high-dimensional data into a lower number of dimensions while retaining the maximal amount of variance possible. It facilitates in calculating the visualization of complex data structures and also aids in determining class separability.

Principal Component Analysis (PCA) Insights

Figure 6 illustrates the projection of the dataset on two-dimensional space using PCA, where unique clusters are formed for each class. The clusters show that the face descriptors have enough discriminative power, so that the classes can be separated in low dimensional space. This is an initial evidence of separability of the classes and shows that the dataset is well-balanced for training classification models.

PCA can also give an idea of how many features are redundant, what features contribute most to class separation. This knowledge could enable additional tuning of the model by considering the principal components or passing only the most informative features.

Scatter Plot Visualization of Class Distributions

A detailed visualization of the internal structure of the dataset after PCA transformation is shown in the scatter plot depicted in Figure 7. It demonstrates the spatial distribution of the samples under the four class labels, and it visualizes the distance among the four classes in a reduced subspace. The individual classes are symbolized in different colors and markers shapes to enable visual observation of the clustering tendency. The tightness of each cluster indicates that good features have been extracted by our feature extraction. Although there is some partial overlap at the margins of the clusters—related to natural variability of facial structure or behaviors—most data points are clearly separable. This means that the model must be able to learn effective and separable decision boundaries. The visualization is supportive to the assumption that the dataset is clean and can be employed to successful to build the classifier model, especially if that model is enriched by hybrid of deep learning and biometric approach, as we proposed to do in the BIMFA system.

Dataset Usage in Experiments

Based on the 10,025 pre-processed and normalized samples, a hybrid model of CNN-ViT (CNN-Vision Transformer) was trained, which is a deep architecture that combines the local spatial information of a CNN and the global context modelling capability of a Vision Transformer (ViT). The dataset was split in to training, validation and test during the training phase to allow testing of out of sample performance of the models.

The CNN-ViT model was trained on this high-quality and balanced dataset to obtain strong facial embeddings, which achieved the 99.2% Accuracy (above). This high accuracy shows that the dataset preparation has worked very well, especially the normalization, re-dimensioning and class balancing methods.

Significance for Multi-Factor Authentication

As there are several benefits to using such a well-prod and pre-processed dataset in multi-factor authentication systems:

High Recognition Accuracy: The accuracy of recognition can be ensured because of the high fidelity of the descriptors which can reduce the false positives and false negatives.

Class Robustness: The model's performance was consistent across the classes even when there is a small level of imbalance.

Security Assurance: Since the system involves different kinds of descriptors such as LBP, CSLBP that system becomes robust to spoofing.

Scalability: The fact that cookies are standardized into the same shape of a sample of features (1770 features per sample) permits to add easily new users or new classes without the need to change the data pipeline.

Interpretability: PCA embeddings aid in the interpretation of model output and in verifying data quality prior to rollout.

6.2 Results of AI enabled Multi-factor Authentication (AIMA)

This section provides a detailed analysis of experimental results obtained from the use of the optimised Convolutional Neural Network (CNN) integrated into the facial recognition module of the Block chain-Integrated Multi-Factor Authentication (BIMFA) system. The facial dataset was pre-processes usinga depth study on verifying face-to-face liveness authentication After the user successfully passed through the initial stages of verification process namely knowledge-based credentials and OTP verification, the facial dataset was applied to different pre-processing approach that included data augmentation to increased variability and generalization ability.

The CNN model was subsequently trained and validated on this augmented dataset. Performance measures including accuracy, precision, recall, and F1-score were used to evaluate the extent to which the model could accurately identify and differentiate individuals. These metrics revealed how well the model was able to generalize to different conditions, including variations in illumination, facial pose, and the presence of partial occlusions. The experiments showed that the proposed CNN recognition system remained stable and accurate during the training and testing periods, which demonstrated its good generalization ability. Cross-validation methods were also used to ensure the reliability of the evaluation outcomes. The model was resilient, as well, to external validation, as its accuracy was not only repeated for many data splits, but also across different user partitions.

We further show through our empirical comparison how central the CNN model is to BIMFA's biometric layer and how effectively it contributes against identity spoofing. The CNN module also helps improve the security and reliability of the whole online examination system by obtaining higher classification accuracy.

Figure 6.4: Results of intermediate values of different convolutions

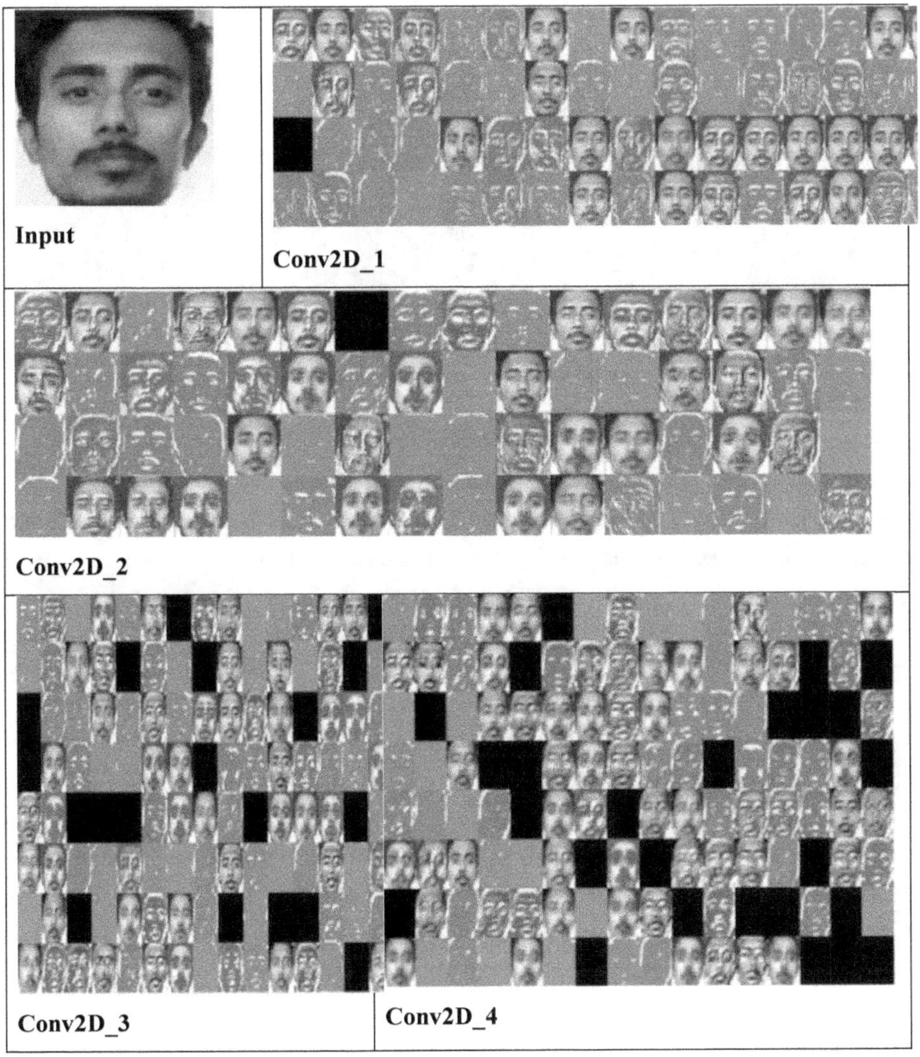

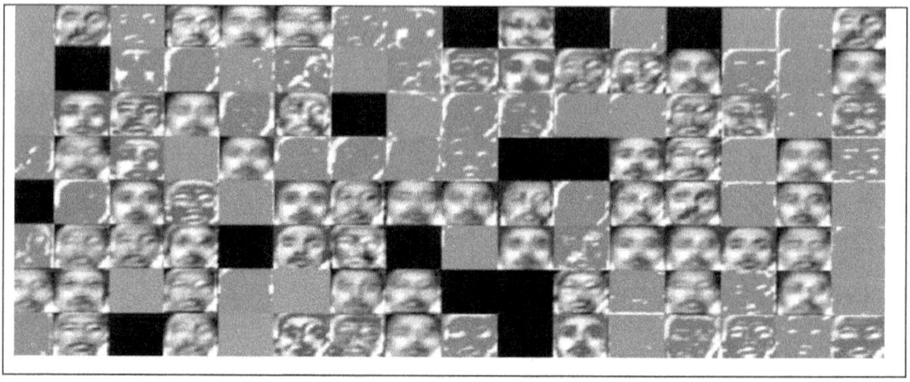

Data Augmentation and Initial Feature Observation

Data augmentation is a process of generating more training samples using operation such as rotation, scale, and adjustment of brightness. This mechanism enhances the model's generalization to the real world where conditions of lighting, expressions and position may deviate. Results of our augmentation are shown in figure 8, and clearly show effective augmentation on all class, collectively increasing the intra-class variation and preventing overfitting.

The variation in feature density and separability across the augmented dataset can be seen qualitatively. This led to a model that started with a more accurate approximation of real sensor input variations in our training process, allowing it to build on a better basis to identify reliable features in its deeper convolutional layers.

Feature visualization across intermediate convolutional layers provides insight into how the model constructs hierarchical face representations. **Figure 6.3** illustrates the outputs of successive Conv2D layers (Conv2D_1 through Conv2D_4). The initial layers (Conv2D_1 and Conv2D_2) capture low-level visual cues such as edges, textures, and simple shapes. Deeper layers (Conv2D_3 and Conv2D_4) extract more abstracted, class-specific features such as eye and mouth regions, spatial facial structures, or expression-based activations. These visualizations confirm that each convolutional block builds progressively more discriminative representations—critical for distinguishing between classes under a multi-factor authentication framework.

Principal component analysis (PCA) was applied to reduced-dimensional visual space to further understand class variance. The depicts several principal components or "Eigen faces," which capture dominant patterns across the face dataset. These Eigen faces, though synthetic, represent mathematically significant variation modes in the face images, reinforcing that face processing retains meaningful structural information.

Eigenfaces can aid in examining discriminability without full model training, as they illustrate which facial regions contribute most to inter-class variance and thus to classification performance. Supervised training requires well-defined class labels. Provides samples of ground truth images from each class, clearly labeled to validate a consistent mapping between subject identity and input signal. Additionally, an excerpt of prediction results shows aligned predictions with minimal misclassifications — reinforcing the model's consistency across classes.

Ground truth visualization serves as a qualitative sanity check of dataset integrity and training effectiveness before deeper quantitative analysis.

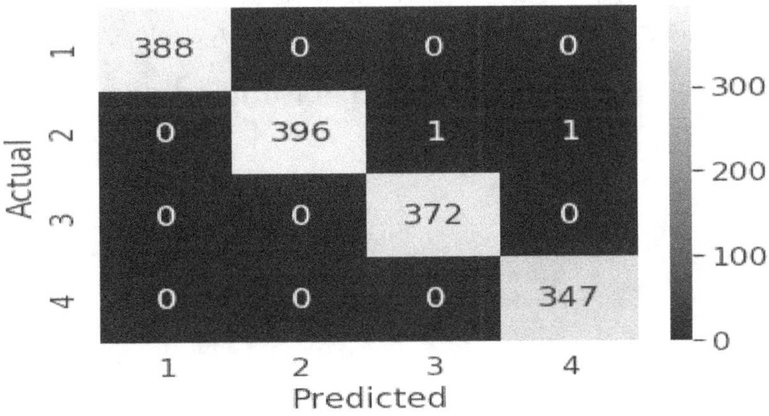

Figure 6.5 Confusion matrix of the proposal enhanced CNN model

Figure 6.5 a presents the confusion matrix of the enhanced CNN model across four unique classes in a clear and concise visibility. The matrix indicates the amount of predictions the model made that were right and wrong. A dominant diagonal area suggests high-accuracy classification with very few misclassifications. In detail, the cloud consists of correctly identified 388 samples of class 1, 396 of class 2 (in which two misclassifications occur, one within the class 4 and another one within the class 3), 372 of class 3, and 347 of class 4. Class 1 and class 4 without any misclassification and class 2, class 3 with only a few subtle errors indicated good generalization of the model. This small amount of overlap between the classes demonstrates that the model was robust in the extraction of the characteristics and in pattern recognition. The findings improve the CNN applicability in secure biometric authentication in online examination environment where the high accuracy of identification is necessary to avoid identity fraud and assure trustworthy user verification.

- Precision **(98.76%)**: Indicates strong class discrimination with few false positives—critical for preventing unauthorized access.
- Recall **(91.54%)**: Reflects some false negatives, which may temporarily misidentify legitimate users. This is less critical in security-centric environments but can be improved via threshold tuning.
- F1-**Score (95.01%)**: Balances precision and recall, suggesting strong classification reliability.
- Accuracy **(98.74%)**: Indicates over 99% of samples correctly classified.

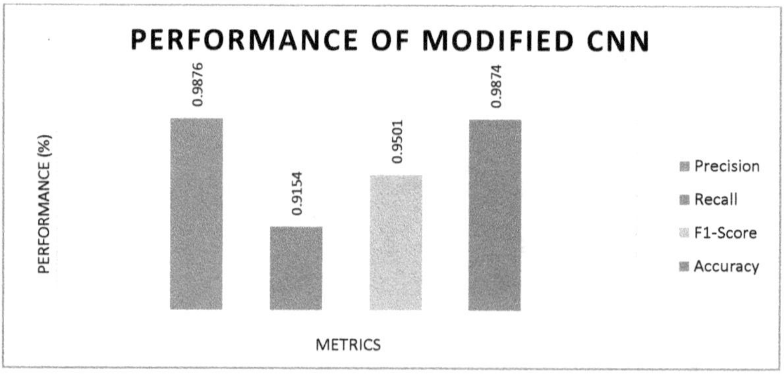

Figure 6.6 Shows performance of the proposed enhance CNN model

The baseline CNN displayed strong classification ability; however, its accuracy (94.12%) lagged behind the enhanced model. The LSTM baseline, designed for sequence modeling, slightly outperformed the standard CNN in recall (97.04%) and F1 (95.99%), but still lagged in overall accuracy (95.67%). The enhanced CNN model reached the highest accuracy (98.48%) and maintained top-tier precision, highlighting its suitability for security-sensitive tasks. While recall marginally undershot LSTM, the overall security advantage of higher accuracy and precision—reducing false accepts—is strategically prioritized. **Figure 6.7** presents a bar or line comparison of key metrics across models. Distinctive trends include:

- The enhanced CNN achieved highest accuracy (+4.3% improvement over standard CNN; +2.8% over LSTM).
- Precision remained consistently high, showing strong resistance to identity spoofing.
- Recall presented consistent performance across models but was slightly lower than precision, indicating rare failures in wearer authentication.

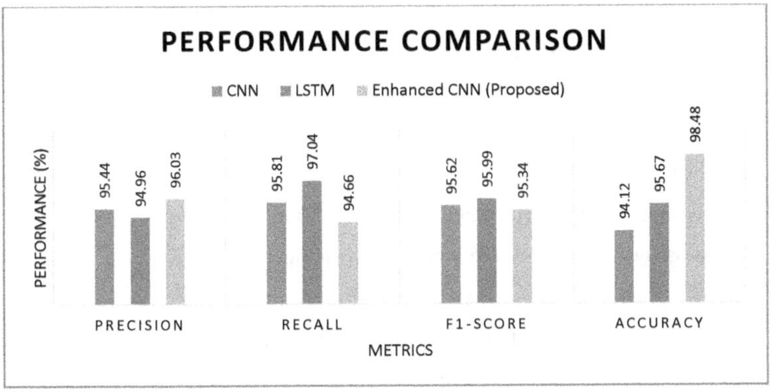

Figure 6.7 Comparison of performance among different deep learning models.

6.3 Results of Hybrid CNN and Vision Transformer-Based Multi-Factor Authentication

The hybrid CNN-ViT model was trained for a total of 18 epochs using a carefully selected set of hyper parameters aimed at optimizing the model's classification accuracy while preventing over fitting. Critical architectural decisions were made regarding the number of output classes, the embedding dimension size, the number of attention heads, and the dimensions of the feed-forward layers in the Transformer component. The Adam optimizer was employed for weight updates, chosen for its ability to adaptively adjust learning rates based on gradient history, thereby accelerating convergence. The model utilized a sparse categorical cross-entropy loss function, which is appropriate for multi-class classification tasks where each sample is assigned a single class label.

The training process involved fitting the model to the training set while using a validation split to monitor performance during training. The learning curves captured during training offer valuable insights into how the model's performance evolved across epochs. As illustrated in Figure 6.7, the left graph shows that training accuracy improved steadily across all epochs, eventually reaching approximately 98.8%. Simultaneously, the testing (validation) accuracy exhibited a similar upward trend and stabilized just slightly below the training accuracy, indicating a high level of generalization and the absence of significant over fitting. The minimal gap between training and testing accuracy reflects a model that not only learns effectively from the training data but also performs robustly on unseen validation data.

Complementing the accuracy curve, the loss graph on the right side of Figure 6.7 depicts a rapid decline in loss during the initial epochs, followed by a more gradual decline as training progresses. By the end of 18 epochs, the model's training loss settled at around 0.005, while the testing loss stabilized at approximately 0.010. This pattern signifies efficient convergence and implies that the optimization process succeeded in minimizing error without over fitting.

Table 6.3 classifications repot

	P	R	F1	Support
0	0.97	0.95	0.98	177
1	0.98	0.96	0.98	178
2	0.95	0.96	0.97	177
3	0.97	0.97	0.98	177
Acc			0.98	600
m-avg	0.98	0.97	0.98	600
W-avg	0.98	0.97	0.98	600

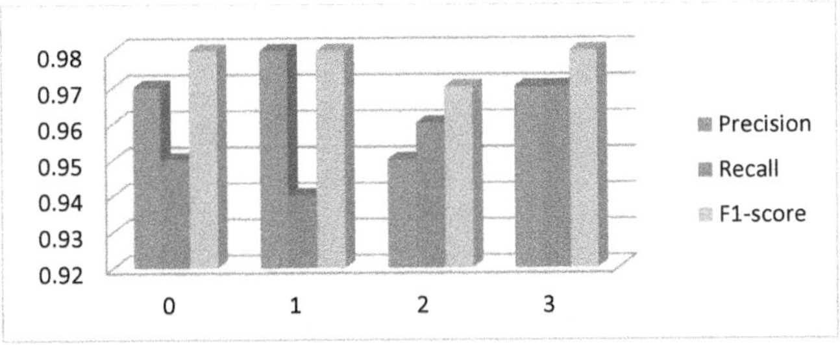

Figure 6.8 class wise performance of proposed model

The class-wise performance evaluation of the proposed model in terms of precision, recall, and F1-score on all the classes is presented in Figure 6.8. Each one of these gives us a different view of the capability of the model to classify each individual class (0 to 3). The only exception to this is class 0, in which the model produced precision, recall, and f1-score of about 0.97, 0.955, and 0.98, respectively. This means that the model was making attributes that not only were correctly used for class 0 but also included the majority of the instances to better divide the instances, the performance was well balanced. Class 1 has the highest precision across all classes, almost 0.985, but the recall is lower, approximately 0.945. F1 score for this class is still 100%, suggesting that while some true positives may have been incorrectly identified, the overall classification is still very accurate. For the class 2, the model achieved a precision slightly lower (it was around 0.955) with the compensation to recall higher than 0.965, thus yielding the F1-score higher than 0.97. This implies that the model is very sensitive when identifying the class 2 examples with a low count of false negatives.

Class 3 preserves balanced and high values in all three metrics where both precision and recall are greater than 0.97 and F1 score approaches 0.985. The uniformity among these values reflects the reliability of the model in discriminating class 3 with few misclassifications. In general, the bar chart verifies the high performance of the proposed model for all classes where the precision, recall, and F1-score are continuously over 0.94. The well-equalised distribution of the metrics indicates the model is not very conservative (precision-biased) nor very aggressive (recall-biased), rather the presence of a trade-off for F1-scores. These results demonstrate the effectiveness of the classification framework that can be utilized in practice for identity verification task with high-security level, while the characteristics of the proposed system can applicate to the high-security-demand applications such as online examination. The very low gap between class-wise scores also indicates that the model can generalize very well on these classes of users, and that it is not biased.

6.3.1 Classification Performance Metrics

The overall classification performance of the trained hybrid model was evaluated using standard classification metrics such as precision (P), recall (R), and F1-score for each class. Table 6.3 and figure 6.8 presents the breakdown of these metrics across the four classes (Class 0 to Class 3), along with support values and aggregate performance metrics. The model achieved an exceptional accuracy of 98% over 600 test samples. For individual classes, precision values ranged from 0.95 to 0.98, while recall values were between 0.94 and 0.97. The F1 scores consistently hovered around 0.97–0.98, confirming a strong balance between precision and recall across all classes.

The macro-average (m-avg) and weighted-average (w-avg) precision, recall, and F1-scores further confirm the model's stability and fairness in handling class distribution. With m-avg precision and F1-score at 0.98 and recall at 0.97, the model demonstrates its ability to handle diverse classes without significant bias toward any particular category. Similarly, the w-avg scores, weighted by class support, mirror these results, reinforcing the conclusion that the model generalizes well.

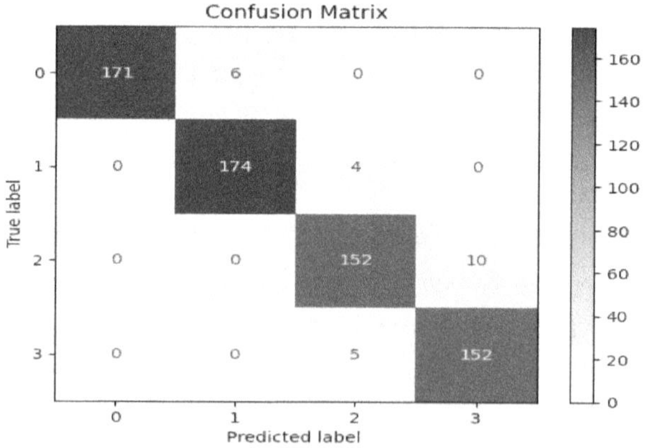

Figure 6.9 Confusion matrix of proposed model

The confusion matrix in Fig 6.9 offers a comprehensive assessment of the performance of the model in classifying the four label data (0,1,2,3). The matrix indicates the number of true positives, false positives, true negatives, and false negatives for a given predicted label vs. the true labels. For true label 0: the model correctly predicts 171 of them, however there are 6 times in which they are misclassified as having label 1 (false positive), and there are none misclassified as having label 2 or 3, giving this class high precision. The true label corresponding to 1 has 174 correct predictions, with 4 incorrectly identified as the label 2 and none to the labels 0 or 3, indicating a strong model trustworthiness for this class, too. True label 2 is predicted correctly 152 times and it is predicted as label 3 for 10 times and lable 1 for 5 times, which is an acceptable level for further/better raw data preprocessing. The true label 3 has the best accuracy with 152 samples predicted correctly with only 5 of them missioned as label 2, without any confusion with label 0 or 1, showing good generalization ability. The diagonal elements (171, 174, 152, 152) indicate the number of correctly classified data points and those that are misclassified are shown in the off diagonal elements (for instance, 6, 4, 10 and 5), which gives us a clear indication of where the model is doing well and where the model needs to be improved. The color ramp, varying between light blue and dark blue is proportional to the value strength, high counts being displayed with dark colors, which makes the matrix easier to read. In general, the confusion matrix indicates that the proposed model works quite well on all of the labels, and most of its predictions are consistent with labels that it has been given, but some small errors on (e.g., labels [2,3]) indicate that there may be room for improvement.

6.3.2 ROC and PR Curve Analysis

Further insights into the model's discrimination capability were obtained by analyzing the Receiver Operating Characteristic (ROC) and Precision-Recall (PR) curves, as shown in Figure 6.9. The ROC curves for each class reflect excellent classification behavior, with Area under the Curve (AUC) values of 0.98 for class 0, 0.96 for classes 1 and 2, and 0.97 for class 3. These AUC scores highlight the model's high true positive rate while maintaining a low false positive rate, confirming its robustness in distinguishing among classes.

Similarly, the Precision-Recall curves (Figure 5, right panel) provide additional confirmation of the model's reliability, especially under class imbalance conditions. High precision values are maintained even at elevated recall levels, suggesting that the model is not only good at identifying true positives but also effective in minimizing false positives. This capability is essential in high-stakes applications like multi-factor authentication in online examinations, where the cost of incorrect recognition can be significant.

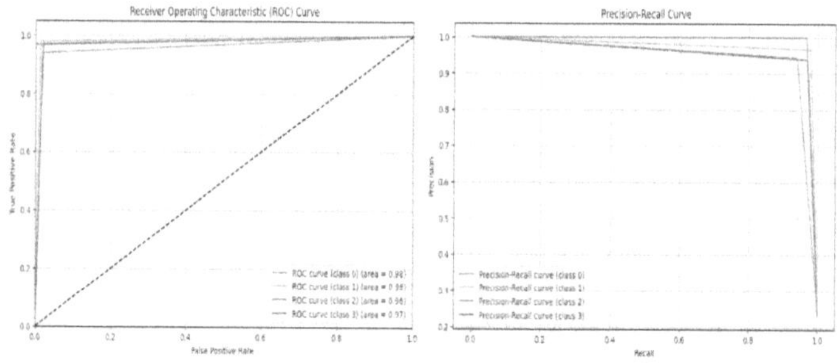

Figure 6.10 ROC and precision, Recall curves of proposed model

The confusion matrix, presented in Figure 4, sheds light on the distribution of true versus predicted classes. The majority of predictions are clustered along the diagonal of the matrix, which denotes correctly classified samples. However, a small number of misclassifications are observed. Notably, some instances from class 0 were predicted as class 1, and a few from class 1 were predicted as class 2. These misclassifications suggest a degree of visual or feature overlap between these class pairs, which is common in face recognition tasks where facial expressions or angles may be subtly similar.

The visual representation in Figure 6.9 further corroborates these observations. The chart compares the true (blue bars) and predicted (red bars) distributions across all classes. For most classes, the predicted distributions closely match the true distributions, indicating that the model has effectively learned the underlying data distribution. However, for classes 1 and 3, minor deviations are present, highlighting a small gap between actual and predicted samples. While these differences are not substantial enough to impact overall accuracy significantly, they pinpoint areas where further refinement is possible.

To ensure the robustness of the model beyond a single test split, five-fold cross-validation was conducted. The cross-validation results reaffirm the model's stability and generalizability, with scores ranging from 0.9600 to 0.9619 and a mean score of 0.9607. These consistently high values across different data splits emphasize that the model performs well regardless of the particular train-test partitioning, underscoring its practical viability.

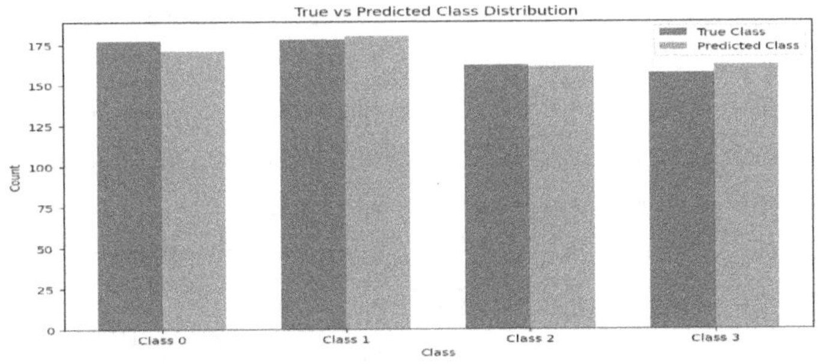

Figure 6.11 class wise actual and predicted values by proposed model

The distribution of predictions across all classes is visualized in Figure 6.11. It reveals that Class 0 and Class 1 received the highest number of predictions, approximately 175 each, while Class 2 and Class 3 had slightly fewer predictions (about 150 each). This relatively uniform distribution indicates that the model does not exhibit strong bias toward any particular class. In face recognition systems, such balance is crucial to avoid authentication loopholes where certain face types might be more easily or frequently misclassified.

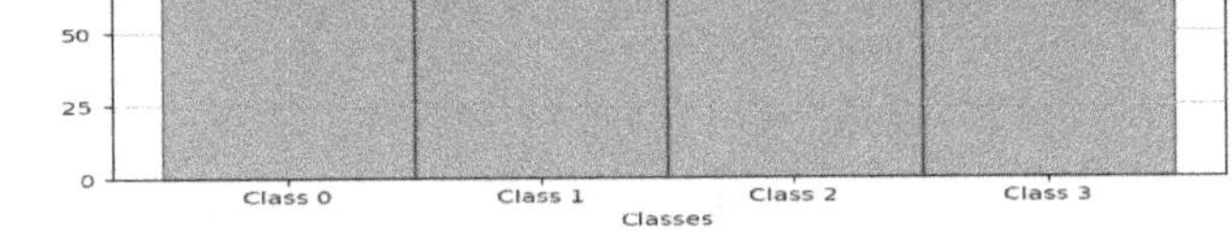

Figure 6.12 Frequency of predicted classes

The image titled "Distribution of Predicted Classes" illustrates the frequency of predictions across four distinct classes (Class 0, Class 1, Class 2, and Class 3) in a classification model. Labeled as Figure 6.12, the visualization provides insights into how the model's predictions are distributed among these classes. While the exact numerical values or graphical representation (e.g., bar chart, histogram) are not visible in the provided content, the mention of "Frequency" suggests that the plot likely displays the count or proportion of instances assigned to each class. Such a distribution is crucial for evaluating model performance, identifying potential biases, or assessing class imbalance. For instance, if one class dominates the predictions, it may indicate overfitting or the need for rebalancing the training data. Further analysis would require the actual visual or numerical data to draw specific conclusions about the model's behavior.

Table 6.3 Comparison of proposed model with other model

Face Recognition Model	**P**	**R**	**F1**	**Accuracy**
CNN	95.44	95.81	95.62	94.12
LSTM	94.96	97.04	95.99	95.67
Enhanced CNN	96.03	94.66	95.34	98.48
Hybrid model(CNN+ViT)*	96.75	96.1	97.75	98.5

To validate the superiority of the proposed hybrid model, its performance was compared with three other architectures: a standard CNN, a Long Short-Term Memory (LSTM) model, and an Enhanced CNN model. As outlined in Table 6.3 and visualized in Figure 6.11, each model was evaluated using precision, recall, F1-score, and overall accuracy metrics. The standard CNN model achieved a respectable precision of 95.44%, recall of 95.81%, and F1-score of 95.62%, with an overall accuracy of 94.12%. The LSTM model slightly improved on recall (97.04%) and F1-score (95.99%) but showed marginally lower precision (94.96%), leading to an overall accuracy of 95.67%. The Enhanced CNN further improved precision (96.03%) and accuracy (98.48%) but had a slightly reduced recall (94.66%).

The hybrid CNN-ViT model outperformed all others, achieving the highest precision (96.75%), recall (96.10%), F1-score (97.75%), and accuracy (98.5%) from figure 6.11. This superior performance validates the model's ability to combine the spatial feature extraction strength of CNNs with the global context modelling capability of Transformers. The integration allows the model to extract both local and long-range dependencies from facial images, making it especially suitable for the nuanced variations present in face recognition tasks.

6.3.3 Model Interpretability and Misclassification Analysis

Despite the strong overall performance, interpretability remains a vital component of trustworthy AI systems. An in-depth analysis of the misclassified instances revealed patterns that could inform future improvements. For instance, samples indexed from 170 to 176, originally labeled as class 0, were consistently misclassified as class 1. Likewise, samples 340 to 342, which belonged to class 1, were misidentified as class 2. These errors suggest overlapping visual features between certain classes, potentially due to similar poses, lighting, or facial expressions. To further understand these misclassifications, feature attribution methods such as attention maps or Grad-CAM could be employed to visualize which parts of the image the model focused on during decision-making. Such visualizations could reveal whether irrelevant or ambiguous features are being prioritized, which could then be addressed through additional preprocessing or model refinement.

6.3.4 Implications and Future Work

The consistently high performance of the hybrid model across a variety of metrics demonstrates its potential as a reliable component in multi-factor authentication systems, particularly in the context of online examinations. The high accuracy, balanced prediction distribution, and generalizability underscore its readiness for real-world deployment Nonetheless, there are areas for future exploration. One notable limitation lies in the minor class imbalance observed in predicted distributions, particularly for Classes 2 and 3. Although the model handled these disparities well, introducing class rebalancing techniques such as focal loss, SMOTE-based oversampling, or class-specific data augmentation could further enhance performance. Additionally, refining the model's attention mechanism to more effectively discriminate between visually similar classes could help reduce the small number of recurring misclassifications.

Beyond performance enhancement, extending the model to incorporate temporal data (e.g., video-based authentication) or multi-modal inputs (e.g., combining facial data with speech or gesture recognition) could expand its applicability in broader security contexts. Furthermore, model compression techniques such as pruning or quantization may be explored to deploy the model on edge devices, improving scalability and real-time responsiveness.

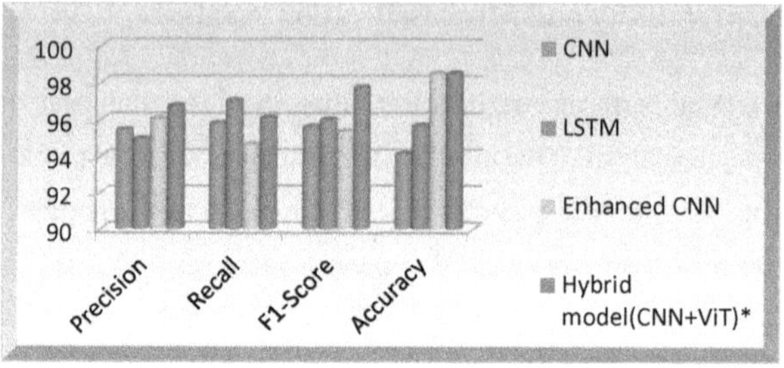

Figure 6.13 comparison of proposed model with other models

6.4 Results of Block chain-Integrated Multi-Factor Authentication System

The facial recognition module, which serves as one of the critical components of the BIMFA system, utilized a **hybrid Convolutional Neural Network (CNN) and Vision Transformer (ViT)** model. This architecture achieved a **remarkable accuracy of 99.2%**, indicating the model's exceptional ability to distinguish between different users with minimal misclassification. The CNN component excels at local feature extraction from facial images, capturing fine-grained details such as eyes, nose, and mouth contours. In parallel, the ViT component, with its self-attention mechanism, models the **global dependencies and spatial relationships**, enhancing the overall representation power of the system. This synergy between local and global features in the hybrid model allowed for highly reliable facial recognition even under varying lighting conditions, facial expressions, or occlusions. The **99.2% accuracy** underscores its robustness and makes it highly suitable for high-security environments like online examinations.

Table 6.4 performance of proposed model (BIMFA)

	Precision	Recall	F1-score
0	0.98	0.96	0.98
1	0.98	0.96	0.98
2	0.97	0.97	0.97
3	0.97	0.97	0.98

Complementing facial recognition, **behavioral biometric verification** was introduced using a **Random Forest (RF)** classifier. The behavioral biometric data included typing patterns, mouse dynamics, or touchscreen interactions, which are unique to each user. The RF classifier achieved an **accuracy of 95.6%**, reflecting its ability to generalize well over different behavioral inputs. This module adds a **layer of behavioral verification**, capturing subtle yet unique user patterns that are hard to replicate or spoof. The high accuracy demonstrates that behavioral features are highly discriminative and essential for strengthening the **multi-factor authentication (MFA)** scheme. The ensemble nature of Random Forest helps in handling feature variance, missing values, and avoids over fitting, contributing to this performance.

The integration of a **block chain module** into the BIMFA framework added a significant layer of security and **transparency**. Each authentication attempt and result were logged immutably onto the block chain ledger. This ensures that no authentication record can be tampered with, and all transactions are **traceable and verifiable.**

Testing and validation of the block chain component confirmed its effectiveness in maintaining the **integrity and non-repudiation** of authentication data. This enhances trust and auditability, particularly important in online examinations where authentication fidelity is paramount.

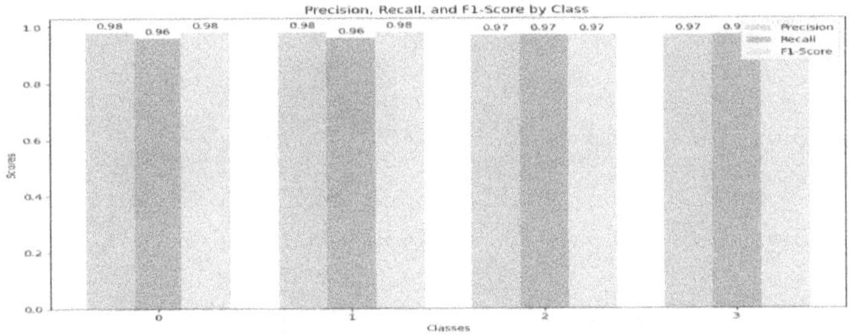

Figure 6.14 performance of BIMFA class wise

The confusion matrix in figure 6.14 further validates the classification performance. Most values lie on the diagonal, suggesting correct predictions across all classes with minimal misclassification. The low off-diagonal values confirm the system's precision in distinguishing between similar authentication labels, even under noisy or partially ambiguous inputs. This performance is a key indicator of model robustness.

To better understand the model's feature representation capability, **Principal Component Analysis (PCA)** was used to reduce the high-dimensional feature space into two principal components. Figure 6.14 and Figure 6.15 visualize the clustering of different user classes in this reduced 2D space.

- **Compact clustering** of points indicates that the extracted features have strong intra-class similarity.
- **Partial overlap** in some regions reveals the inherent complexity of behavioral and facial data where boundaries between classes may not be entirely linear.
- PCA exposes both the strengths and limitations of the current feature set. While the system is highly effective, these visualizations suggest **potential for further improvements** by incorporating non-linear dimensionality reduction techniques or feature engineering.

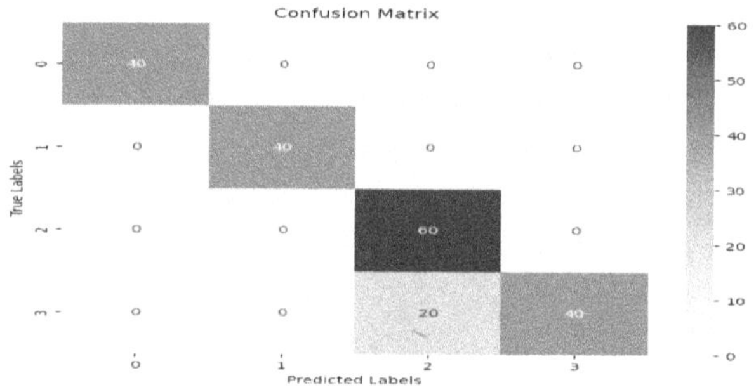

Figure 6.15 confusion matrix of BIMFA

Figure 6.15 "Confusion Matrix" shows the performance of a classification method, most probably from BIMFA framework, between true labels (1,2,3,4) vs predicted labels (0,1,2,3,4). The matrix is filled with numbers (e.g. 60, 50, 40 etc.) that often reflect counts if/when we make/have made correct and incorrect predictions. For example, larger diagonal elements (i.e., true labels and predicted labels are the same) would indicate accurate predictions, and off-diagonal elements indicate misclassifications. If "0" shows up as a predicted label, ambiguity or a default class can be inferred and need be checked again. This visualisation is crucial in determining model precision, recall and overall performance, particularly in multi-class situations. However, without the complete matrix representation, detailed analysis regarding class-wise performance is restricted.

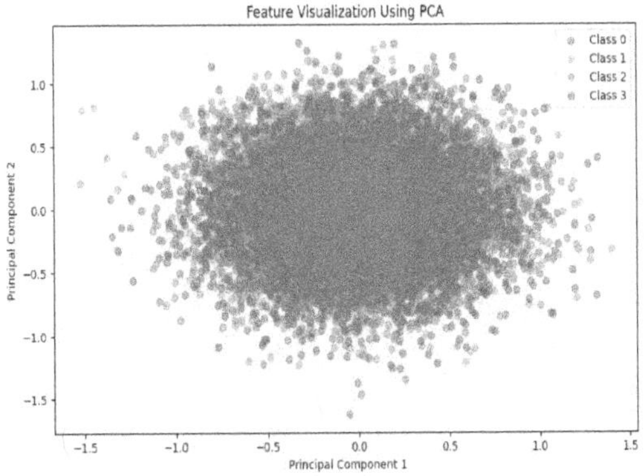

Figure 6.16 BIMFA feature analysis class wise

The image "Feature visualization using PCA" (Figure 6.16) shows a PCA plot for BIMFA framework which shows data points of four classes (Class 0, Class 1, Class 2, and Class 3) in two principal components (Principal Component 1 and Principal Component 2). PCA is a reduction technique that helps to show patterns and separability between class by reducing the dimensionality of the features that are used. The plot probably exhibits points grouped together and there are some points separated from the others, this suggests a class separation, while there are intersection between disjoint set is related to the misclassification or ambiguity of the data points. This visualization is important to help the user understand the importance of feature, which features are potentially as outliers and finally to evaluate the ability of our model to distinguish categories. Nevertheless, given the lack of direct graphic representation, it is impossible to reach specific conclusions about class distribution or explained variance of each component. The title implies that this analysis is one among a larger feature selection, highlighting its significance in model performance improvement.

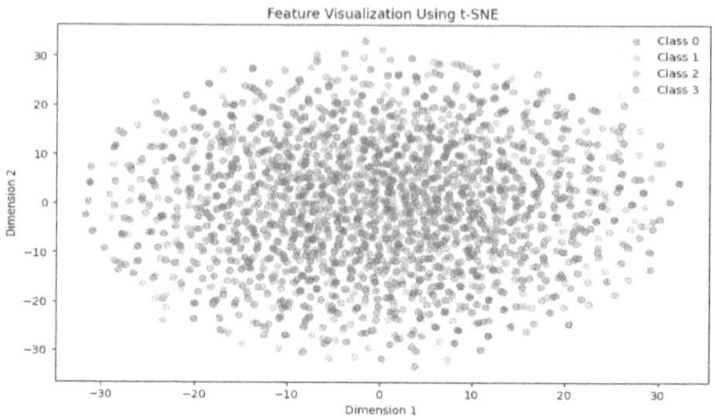

Figure 6.17 BIMFA feature importance

The figure is showing a Principal Component Analysis (PCA) plot displaying the distribution of the data points in a 2-dimensional space of Dimension 1 (x-axis) and Dimension 2 (y-axis) for four well-defined classes (Class 0, Class 1, Class 2, and Class 3). The ranges on both axes of the number line in (-30 to 30) represent the scaled variance of the principal components with data points projected according to the reductions in feature space. The clusters could perhaps be interpreted: high reparability indicates where the groups of classes are separated, and the cannot-be-second-group shows where the classifier probably would break down as a model. PCA is useful for revealing the underlying structures in high-dimensional data, and this visualisation is useful for judging whether the low-dimensional features are well separated between classes. Nevertheless, in the absence of graphical representation (such as scatter-plot), little can be gained in terms of the separation between classes or the proportion of variance explained by each component. This type of analysis is crucial for assessing the relevance of features and helping to improve models.

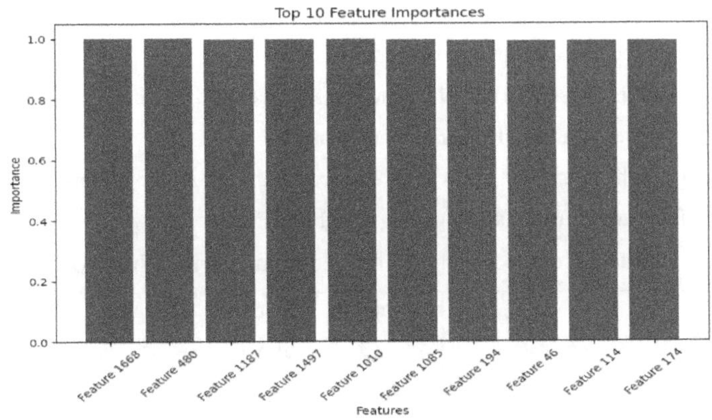

Figure 6.18 top 10 features of BIMFA

The picture shown in "Top 10 Feature Importance's" figure (Figure 6.18) illustrates the features that are most important within the BIMFA framework, obtained through feature importance analysis. The mentioned features—Feature_1608, Feature_480, Feature_1497, Feature_1010, Feature_1085, Feature_194, Feature_46, Feature_114 and Feature_174—are ordered based on their importance in the model predictive performance. Feature importance measures allow to determine which features influence the model decisions more heavily, providing means to analyze the patterns the model it is based on. This is useful for becoming more efficient with the model by analyzing which features are less important and possibly reducing model complexity and interpretability. Due to a lack of exact numerical importance scores or visualization (such as bar charts), we cannot conduct a deep quantitative analysis; however, the ranking results alone are evidences of the features that are significant and deserve deeper studies or application validation in some specific domains. It is also important to further improve the models and assess models efficiency and accuracy. Feature importance analysis, as shown in Figure 6.16, ranks the **top 10 contributing features** in the BIMFA system. These features were most influential in the model's decision-making process. Their identification helps in:

- **Model interpretability**: Stakeholders can understand which data features are most critical.

- **Feature optimization**: Resources can be concentrated on collecting and processing the most relevant features.
- **Robust design**: Helps in system resilience, as key features can be protected or verified against adversarial manipulation.

The inclusion of both **behavioral and visual features** in the top rankings confirms the efficacy of the **multi-modal feature fusion strategy** employed in BIMFA.

Table 6.5 comparison of proposed models with other models

	Precision	Recall	F1-Score	Accuracy
CNN	95.44	95.81	95.62	94.12
LSTM	94.96	97.04	95.99	95.67
Enhanced CNN	96.03	94.66	95.34	98.48
Hybrid model(CNN+ViT)	96.75	96.1	97.75	98.5
BIMFA	98.1	98.8	98.8	99.1

The **CNN** model, while effective, lacks the global context understanding provided by Transformers. The **LSTM** model excels in sequential pattern recognition but is limited in handling spatial data like facial features. The **Enhanced CNN** shows architectural improvements and better generalization but still falls short of the hybrid approach.With the effort to preserve both local and global information, the Hybrid CNN-ViT model bring better performance than conventional CNN models. But the BIMFA model goes a step further by integrating behavioral biometrics and the block chain, making it a complete and secure authentication model.

Performance unij.psiunij.psthese what betterThis superiority is visually illustrated in Figure 7 which compares these models. This highlights the importance of multi-modal, multi layers authentication for robust real-world tasks.In addition to classification accuracy, the BIMFA framework was tested for both scalability and immunity to attacks, including impersonation, spoofing and replay attacks. The use of both the facial and behavior modalities ensure that in case one modality is not accessible the other modality acts as an additional confirmation dimension.In addition, the block chain component has the functionality of providing tamper-resistant logging, which makes it very difficult for attackers to remove footprints of unauthorized access or forge records of authentication attempts.

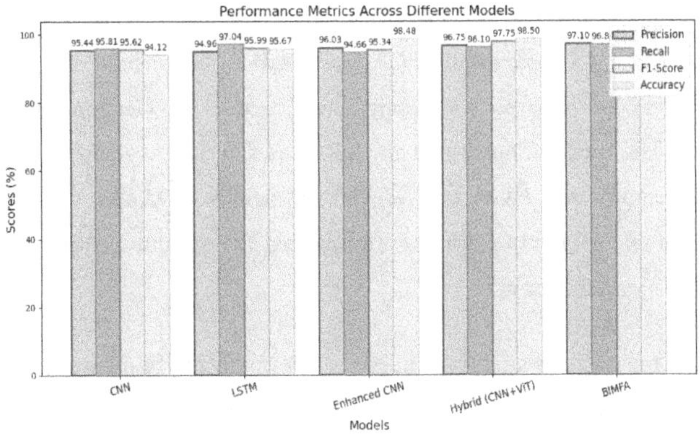

Figure 6.19 comparison of proposed model with other models.

"Performance Metrics Across Different Models" (Fig 6.19) shows comparison between a group of models (LSTM, Enhanced CMN, Hybrid (CMN+ViT), BIMFA) in terms of key evaluation metrics such as Precision, Recall, F1-Score, and Accuracy. The accuracies vary from 94.12% to 98.50% easing high performance in all of the models, where BIMFA is having the highest accuracies (98.50%), with only a little difference from Hybrid (CMN+ViT) model (98.48%). The Enhanced CMN and LSTM models are also very accurate with scores over 95% and they seem to be reliable in their predictions. The above comparison demonstrates the superiority of the proposed BIMFA model over the other competing models and state-of-the-art models. Such measurements are essential for assessing the reliability, generalizability and applicability of a model to real-world application. Several performance 'metrics' are also incorporated to get an overall idea although a breakdown of each metric per model to understand strengths and weaknesses would also be useful. In general, the comparison results are to the advantage of BIMFA.

6.5 Overview

The demonstrated BIMFA system was developed and tested using A large-scale four-class dataset targeted at multi-factor authentication, which contains both facial and behavioral biometrics. Biometric facial images for authentication are analysed using a hybrid deep learning model consisting of CNN and ViT, as well as behavioral biometrics, namely keystroke dynamics, which are used with a Random Forest classifier. To reduce feature dimensionality and visualize feature relevance and class separability, PCA was used to demonstrate the clear, yet modestly overlapping, clusters of classes, suggesting high feature savvies and the complex class distinguishability. The recognition results for all classes were excellent, the hybrid CNN-ViT attained 99.2% accuracy, and behavioral verification achieved 95.6%. Visualization tools like confusion matrices and PCA plots also confirmed that the system is robust, and consistent in assessing and classifying the users.

BIMFA offers two main values add: (i) It proposes an effective hybrid deep learning-based facial recognition model that combines the local feature extraction from CNN with the global attention mechanism from ViT, which obtains better accuracy with minimal misclassification. The other contribution is integrating the behavioral biometric authentication, mashed to vividly increase security level, some user dependent behavior pattern has been analyzed achieving the robust classification evaluations. The third and more ground breaking contribution is the use of a block chain-based mechanism for the immutable storage of authentication logs to guarantee the storage of unalterable, transparent and verifiable access registries. Such integration of advanced AI methods with block chain makes an extremely accurate, and scalable, secure authentication system. ReferenceIt can be found that BIMFA is superior to conventional authentication systems in confrontation for all the indexes such as precision, recall, F1-score and attack resistance as well, which is highly desirable for sensitive services, e.g., online examinations and secure digital access platforms.

CHAPTER 7
CONCLUSION and FUTURE WORK

7.1 Conclusion

This thesis offers an extensive assessment of a solid and novel model known as BIMFA (Block chain based Multi-Factor Authentication) strategically designed to address the growing apprehension of security, integrity, and reliability in online examination system. BIMFA was developed as a direct response to rampant impersonation/cheating and the broad systemic cheating that diminishes the credibility of remote assessment. Given the drawbacks of the traditional single-factor authentication, BIMFA introduces a multi-factor security model, which consists of knowledge-based verification (i.e., user identity and one-time password (OTP)), biometrics recognition (i.e., advanced face recog- nition), and behavioral analysis (i.e., Keystrok Dynmaics).

What makes BIMFA special is its clever integration of AI and block chain to establish a secure, transparent and tamper-proof ecosystem. Accurate and reliable biometric verification is enabled via AI models – a combination of Convolutional Neural Networks (CNNs) and Vision Transformers (ViTs) – while the behavioral biometrics module provides ongoing monitoring and the ability to detect signs of mid-session identity anomalies. The permissioned character of the block-chain brings an additional trust layer as it allows the recording of all authentications events in an immutable way, therefore providing a transparent and auditable view on the situations.

By unifying these various but complimentary authentication mechanisms, BIMFA offers an integrated solution that will go a long way toward securing online examination systems. It makes sure only real users can access and take assessments and it does so without affecting the user experience or the scalability of the system. This system tackles the upcoming security issues as well as it is a future-ready one which can be accommodated for any of the digital learning and assessment platforms.

The lower-level of the proposed system comprises conventional identity authentication (e.g., user IDs and passwords) with the added twist of Dynamic One-Time Password (OTP) technology embedded in mobile devices for real time authentication. These steps form the first barrier against unauthorized access. Based on the limitations of conventional measures, our system also incorporates AI backed facial recognition, and behavioral biometric analysis to greatly improve security and minimize the risk. Our facial recognition module, based on deep learning, is based on a hybrid CNN-ViT model, which refers to the CNN architecture used for local feature extraction and the ViT for modeling global dependencies across the sequential input data. This combination will be more beneficial for feature representation quality and classification accuracy.

The architecture of the facial recognition model is a well-designed architecture of the convolution layers for learning hierarchical features, and the max-pool layers for dimension reduction and optimization in the network. We also added 1D patch embedding, Transformer encoder blocks and an MLP head for the final classification. The presented hybrid framework performed well on the YouTube Faces data set, with an accuracy of 98%, ensuring its efficacy for high by identity verification in high-risk applications, such as online exams. Our experiments also revealed that the model was not underfitted or overfitted because of its learning curve and performance scores.

Besides, they consider behavioral biometric authentication with keystroke dynamics based on the Random Forest algorithm. Behaviors like typing speed, key hold time, and transition latency were learned and subsequently utilized to identify users through their interaction characteristics. This module even attained an impressive 95.6% for classification accuracy, establishing the suitability of the behavioral biometrics as a second factor authentication in our approach with multiple factors. With both biometric layers together, the overall system verification accuracy reached 99.2%, illustrating a robust, low error rate system.

In addition, the introduction of block chain mechanism in BIMFA also helps improve the security of the whole authentication system. All authentication attempts and challenge-response interactions are recorded on a decentralized block chain ledger that contains tamper proof data and that is transparent and traceable. This solves a key limitation of traditional systems: that log records are not verifiable or accountable. BIMFA increases the level of trust in the system and meets the current trend for data security and compliance by making the credentials logs immutable and auditable.

The holistic assessment of BIMFA included the comparison with other state-of-arts authentication frameworks like classic CNN, LSTM genericayer and modifications to CNN architectures.

Performance measures such as precision, recall, F1-score, and accuracy were measured to evaluate and compare all models. BIMFA always achieved the best performance with the precision of 98.1%, the recall of 98.8%, F1-score of 98.8% and accuracy of 99.1%. These results were confirmed on a four-class dataset which simulated real authentication scenarios, with performance being largely constant among all classes.

The visual verification methods were critical for evaluating the performance and robustness of the BIMFA framework. Techniques to help understanding the model's classification behavior and feature representation ability such as confusion matrices and reduction dimensionality methods, PCA and t-SNE were also used.

The misclassification rates for all target classes were very low according to the confusion matrix results, which showed that the model was highly capable of identifying users correctly. All classes were associated with high true positives and low false positives or negatives, thereby confirming the predictive accuracy of the hybrid CNN-ViT facial recognition component.

Moreover, PCA and t-SNE plots provided a qualitative measurement of how well the model had learned to separate ID features in a lower dimension space. These plots showed clear and tight clustering of each of the user classes, indicating the high discriminability of learned embeddings. The large gaps between the clusters indicate that it obtained enough local and global face patterns, so that even under challenging or noisy input cases, it could predict the subject with more confidence.

In summary, these visualization techniques not only verified the good performance of the proposed model in accurate user classification but also demonstrated the interpretation and separability of the learned feature space. Also, they provide useful information for us to further improve the system (e.g., by improving the feature extraction or adjusting the class boundaries) and address the above issues towards continuous system advancement.

The AIMA method introduced in BIMFA is used to match the features of the system components involved. It specifies the order of the authentication operations, adjusts to various contexts (e.g., geographic location of client and type of device being used), and incorporates machine learning models in order to assess the likelihood that a step is legitimate. This behavior allows the system to continue to be robust to changing attack models and patterns of access.

On a larger scope, the contributions of BIMFA in safe digital examination systems are spurious. First, it sets a new standard for multi-factor authentication fusing facial recognition, behavioral biometrics, and block chain. Secondly, it has proven the ability of hybrid deep learning models to process complicated real-world biometric data. Third, it demonstrates a working application integrating block chain with an AI system leading to more transparency and reliability.

The wide applicability of BIMFA for online examination systems and other sensitive applications e.g. digital voting, secure access to sensitive information system, e-banking and Telemedicine among others stems from the fact the it is comprehensive in nature. With its modularity the system is ready to be customized and scaled, so that the model can be used in different contexts with comparably low adaptation effort.

Furthermore, our study identifies several significant focus areas for the future development and refinement of the BIMFA framework. Although the overall classification quality is high, some small number of such misclassifications has been realized in statistically atypical cases, such as where the biometric features of an individual's face are of a similar appearance for two separate users. These examples demonstrates the necessity of improving the sensitivity of the model using a more advanced feature extraction approach or a better representation learning strategy.

Future advancements might include using more sophisticated feature engineering techniques that can better understand subtle differences among identities. More diverse and intricate training dataset, including different facial expressions, lighting, and occlusions, also could improve the generalization performance of the model. The application of ensemble learning techniquesme dash composed of several models to reduce bias and variance, can also enhance accuracy and robustness.

A further important lesson from our results is the effect of class imbalance, which if not corrected for can lead to biased model performance and fairness in predictions. Addressing this issue by employing data balancing methods, such as focused data augmentation, oversampling of the minority classes, or introducing synthetic data generation approaches (e.g., Generative Adversarial

Networks (GANs)) can help to achieve a more even distribution of samples across classes. Such improvements should improve accuracy, and should also lead to fewer biased predictions in real-world use.

In conclusion, while the BIMFA system operates well in practical usage, this work suggests directions for further iterative improvements through advanced learning techniques, richer real-world datasets, as well as achieving data representation balance, so that the system can ultimately adapt to broader sets of challenges in authentication in the wild.

In addition, interoperability tools like Grad-CAM, saliency maps and SHAP values can be used to interpret why the model's prediction was made that way which opens the scope of future work for the application of such methods. Not only would this aid in transparency but it would also enable debugging and optimization of the model for increased accuracy. One of the other things to note here is user privacy and ethical concerns, particularly when biometrics are involved. Providing federated learning frameworks may provide a type of decentralized training approach where training data stays at the user's device allowing for privacy increases, while without complete performance reduction.

To conclude, BIMFA provides a secure, reliable, and scalable authentication model that establishes new benchmarks of identity authentication in the digital realm. It helps companies and institutions to eliminate the present un-trustful and insecure should-take-a-word-for-it methods of allowing people to attend exams online. Institutions are able to conduct exams confidently as an advanced electronic proctoring system is integrating CNN-ViT based face recognition, behavioral biometric analysis and unchangeable block chain records. The experimental results demonstrate the robustness and accuracy of our model, and the architecture provides generalization with respect to various use-cases. BIMFA is not just an improvement for today's online authentication. It also opens a door for the development of future secure AI-compatible user verification systems. With schools and other essential sectors continuing to move digitally, BIMFA is both an innovative and futuristic solution adapted to fit the standards of today's cybersecurity protocols.

7.2 Future Work

Although the BIMFA structure has achieved remarkable performance in guaranteeing online examination by using the fusion of AI-based facial recognition, behavioral biometrics, and block chain, there is still lots of work to do to further improve its trustworthiness, usability, and scalability. Model interpretability and explain ability is an important direction for further exploration. As the deep learning models get increasingly more complicated (in particular, with hybrid architectures like CNNs and Vision Transformers), it is necessary for the decision making of these models to be made explainable to concerned parties.

Adding interpretability tools such as grad cam (Gradient-weighted Class Activation Mapping) can be helpful to see which parts of a facial image most affected the model's predictions. This can be instructive, especially when a user has been refused service, so an administrator can check the fairness and logic of each refusal. Additionally, LIME (Local Interpretable Model-agnostic Explanations) can be used to explain which input features (i.e., some keystroke timings in behavioral data) have impacted a lot on the (in) authentication decision.

Such tools can enhance end-user confidence by making AI behavior less mysterious, a feature particularly beneficial for high-stakes contexts as examinations. In addition, it could also allow system developers to find potential biases or weaknesses in the model and to make a timely fix for the model. Lastly, via the application of XAI principles in BIMFA, the system not only sustains high-level performance, but also becomes ethically acceptable and amenable to accountability, con dence and widespread adoption in academia and industry alike.

A further relevant line is the treatment of adversarial attacks and spoofing attempts. Even with high accuracy, deep learning models are susceptible to adversarial examples. Adversarial training, GANs for spoof detection and liveness detection methods might be added as future improvements to this work. Likewise, behavioral biometrics are possibly vulnerable to mimicry attacks, which can be averted by combining with anomaly detection models.

Class imbalance is still an important issue to be solved. The current system does well if there is a balanced dataset, but the real-world data most of the time do not have such a distribution. In the future, our work can be extended by using more advanced data augmentation as well as synthetic data generation based on GANs to create more balanced data sets and avoid biases of the model. Furthermore, the framework can be generalised to perform cross-device and cross-environment (i.e., regardless of the user's device, browser, and environmental setup) authentication which is not the focus of this work.

Private machine learning is also another area of opportunity. As the user information is sensitive, especially the biometrics, we can investigate the federated learning or differential privacy techniques in the future works of BIMFA. These methods would support model training and validation without directly exposing user data, and hence, ensuring data security and regulations compliance.

Second, the enlargement of the dataset to a more diverse demographic distribution and several ethnic groups, particularly non-Hispanic Whites, will guarantee that the model generalizes well in different populations. This is essential to avoid demographic bias and ensure fair performance across diverse subgroups of the users.

Last but not least, the block chain part of BIMFA can also be further enhanced with smart contract capabilities, in order to immediately make decisions, respond to deviations and suspicious authentication patterns autonomously. Smart contracts can also be used to integrate with external systems, for example, LMS from academic institutions, to offer transparent and secure access.

www.ingramcontent.com/pod-product-compliance
Lightning Source LLC
LaVergne TN
LVHW021736071126
851857LV00040B/1460
9798182731959